HERITAGE STUDIES 3

Third Edition

bju press
Greenville, South Carolina

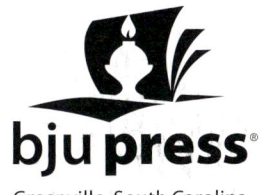

Note
The fact that materials produced by other publishers may be referred to in this volume does not constitute an endorsement of the content or theological position of materials produced by such publishers. Any references and ancillary materials are listed as an aid to the student or the teacher and in an attempt to maintain the accepted academic standards of the publishing industry.

Heritage Studies 3
Third Edition

Author
Brian C. Collins, PhD

Consultants
Marnie Batterman
Eileen Berry
Ethan G. Birney
James R. Davis
Annittia Jackson
Debra White

Bible Integration
Bryan Smith, PhD

Project Editors
Maria S. Dixson
Joey Hoelscher

Page Layout
Bonnijean Marley

Designer
Michael Asire

Cover Design
Elly Kalagayan

Cover Art
Ben Schipper

Cover Photography
Craig Oesterling

Project Coordinator
Kendra Wright Winchester

Illustrators
Paula Cheadle
Sarah Ensminger
Zach Franzen
Preston Gravely
Sandy Mehus
Steve Mitchell
Kathy Pflug
Dave Schuppert
Lynda Slattery
Heather Stanley
Del Thompson

Permissions
Sylvia Gass
Sarah Gundlach

Photograph credits appear on pages 309–11.

Excerpt from text on Dred Scott's headstone, The Dred Scott Heritage Foundation, http://www.thedredscottfoundation.org (page 223)

© 2014, 2020 BJU Press
Greenville, South Carolina 29609
First Edition © 1982 BJU Press
Second Edition © 1997, 1999, 2009 BJU Press

Printed in the United States of America
All rights reserved

ISBN 978-1-62856-883-7

15 14 13 12 11 10 9 8 7 6 5 4 3 2 1

Contents

Chapter

1: Beginnings	2
2: The Constitution	28
3: Presidents and Precedents	48
4: Jefferson and Moving West	76
5: The War of 1812 and National Growth	102
6: Andrew Jackson and Democracy	132
7: Growth in the East	160
8: The United States Spreads West	186
9: A Nation Dividing	212
10: The Civil War	240

Resource Treasury 270

Primary Sources	272
Atlas	280
Geogloss	284
Gazetteer	286
Biographical Dictionary	292
Glossary	296

Index 302

To the Student

History is a story of past events. In this book, you will learn about past events in our country. We can trust God with our history, because God is the One who controls history.

Did you know that . . .
- John Adams was elected as the second president of the United States and was the first to live in the new capital city of Washington, DC?
- The Underground Railroad was created to provide safe places for slaves to hide on their way to freedom?
- Clara Barton risked her life to help wounded soldiers during the Civil War and established the Red Cross which still helps people today?

This year you will learn that some people came to our country so they could worship God freely. You will grow in your understanding of God and how He blessed America in spite of mistakes people made.

1 Beginnings

Focus
America's history began as people looked for freedom and opportunity.

The Great Commission

"Go ye therefore, and teach all nations" (Matthew 28:19). These words of Jesus are called the Great Commission. Jesus **commissioned**, or commanded, His disciples to tell others about Jesus. He told the disciples to teach those who trusted in Him to obey His commands.

The disciples went everywhere preaching the gospel. They went to India, Egypt, and Europe. Many people became Christians. Europe was special because Christianity kept growing there. After many years, most people in Europe called themselves Christians. But not all were true followers of Christ in their hearts and actions. Even so, Christianity was the main religion of Europe.

Another religion started near where Jesus had lived. This religion is called Islam. Its followers are Muslims. The Muslims took over the land of Israel. Christians in Europe thought Muslims should not rule Israel. So the European Christians tried to get Israel back.

Europeans and Trade

The Europeans traded with the Muslims for things the Europeans did not have. These goods often came from India and China. The prices for these goods were high. The goods had to pass through many different traders to get to Europe.

Europeans looked for other ways to get these goods. They built ships to sail around Africa. This way the ships could reach India and China. These places had the same goods for lower prices. The Europeans could then buy and sell the goods to make a profit. A **profit** is the extra money made after paying for goods. But sailing around Africa was long and dangerous.

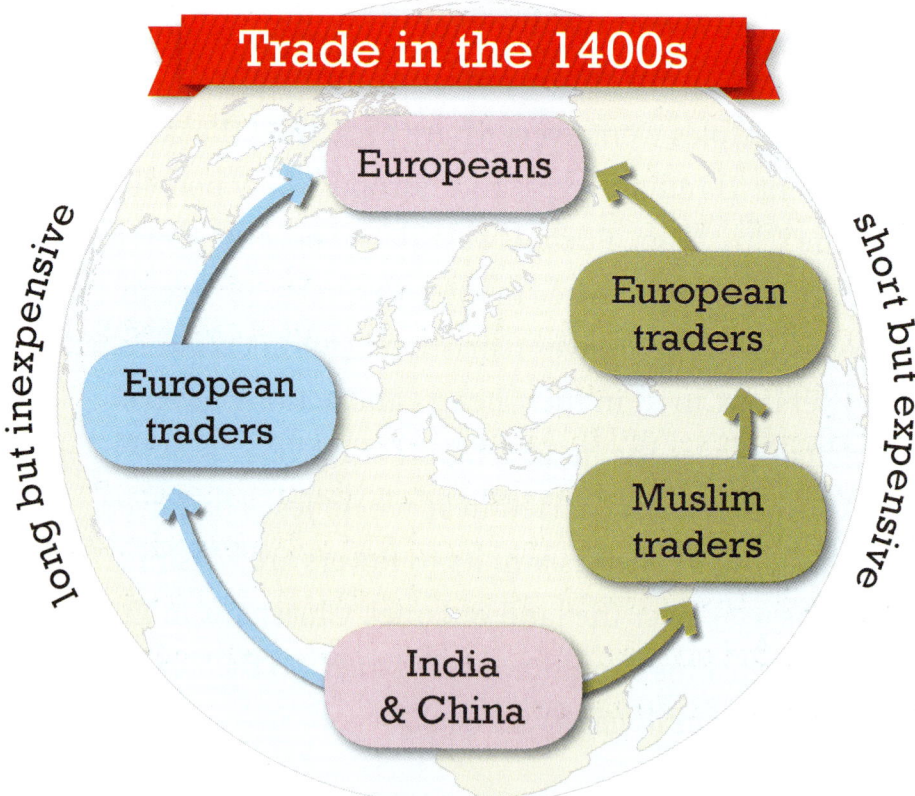

Sailing West

The European traders had sailed east to reach India and China. What if their ships sailed west? Could they still reach these places? Christopher Columbus thought it would be a shorter and safer way. Most people disagreed. They thought the earth was too big for this idea to work. Columbus said the earth was much smaller than people thought.

Columbus sailed on ships similar to this one.

Columbus was determined to sail west. He thought Europeans could make a bigger profit if they sailed in that direction. They could use the money to fight the Muslims and get Israel back. Columbus also thought that this new *route*, or course, could be used to spread Christianity around the world. Isabella, the queen of Spain, agreed to give him money and ships.

Columbus set sail in August 1492. He and his crew arrived at an island in the Caribbean Sea on October 12, **1492**. Columbus named the island **San Salvador**. He called the people there **Indians** because he thought he was near India. He did not know that he had discovered lands that were new to the Europeans.

Columbus sailed from island to island, but he could not find the cities of India. He met with many people. They did not have the goods the Europeans wanted. Columbus was not going to make a big profit.

Columbus wanted the people he met to become Christians. He taught them prayers. He taught them to make the sign of the cross in the air. They learned quickly, and he thought they would become Christians. But he had wrong ideas about how people become Christians. He did wrong to some of the Indians. He captured them and took them back to Spain on his ships.

Columbus was wrong about the size of the earth. He was wrong about where he landed. He mistreated the Indians. However, God is in control of history. In God's plan, **Christopher Columbus** discovered what we now call the Americas.

> Why did Columbus want to sail west?

Columbus mistreated the Indians.

The New World

People in Europe quickly learned that Columbus had found new lands. Europeans called them the New World. Many countries sent explorers to the New World. Some countries sent people to start colonies. England was one of these countries. There were not enough jobs for everyone in England. Some people were sent to prison because they could not pay their bills. Colonies offered people a new start. Wealthy Englishmen bought ships and supplies to send people to the New World. These wealthy men wanted to make a profit through trade. Some of the English wanted to teach the Indians to become Christians. People also went for land to build farms.

The English had tried to form colonies in the New World. But each time, they failed. Finally, the English built a colony called Jamestown. An Indian chief named Powhatan helped the English succeed. His tribes were threatened by other tribes. These tribes traded with French explorers for weapons. Powhatan needed weapons to fight back. So he traded with the English at Jamestown for weapons. This trade helped the English survive.

The Indians and the English did not always treat each other well. Some of the Indians attacked Jamestown. The English then burned some Indian villages and destroyed their food. John Smith, a leader in Jamestown, tried to stop the fighting. The Indians captured Smith, and Powhatan threatened to kill him. But Pocahontas, Powhatan's daughter, begged to spare his life. The Indians finally released Smith.

Later the English captured Pocahontas. They would not free her until Powhatan freed the English captives. Powhatan refused. While Pocahontas lived in Jamestown, she learned the English language. She learned about Jesus and believed what she heard. Pocahontas married John Rolfe, an important man in Jamestown. Pocahontas helped the Indians and the English understand each other better.

John Smith

Jamestown was built as a fort to keep the colonists safe.

The Pilgrims

In England the king ran both the government and the churches. Every church had to follow the king's orders. One group of Englishmen, the Pilgrims, did not like this. They thought the king should not run churches. So the Pilgrims started their own churches. This was against the law.

The Pilgrims wanted freedom to worship God as the Bible taught. To have this freedom, they needed to leave England. They received permission to establish a colony in the New World. They hired a ship called the *Mayflower*. But storms blew the ship off course. The Pilgrims landed north of where they were supposed to live. They decided to stay where they landed.

The Pilgrim leaders knew they needed to establish their own government. They knew that people are not naturally good. God uses government to stop people from acting wickedly. The Pilgrim leaders wrote laws for their colony. These laws were called the **Mayflower Compact**. The Pilgrims founded **Plymouth Colony** in **1620**.

The signing of the Mayflower Compact, painted by an American artist in the late 1800s

The first year in Plymouth was very hard. The Pilgrims did not have enough food or houses. Only about half of those who came on the *Mayflower* lived through the first winter. The Plymouth colony would not have survived without help from the Indians. In the spring, an Indian chief named Samoset met with the Pilgrims. They were amazed that he spoke English. He had learned it from English fishermen. From Samoset the Pilgrims learned that an Indian tribe had once lived in the same area. They were a warlike people who had been killed by a disease.

Only one person from the tribe survived: Squanto. Before the disease came, he had been kidnapped and taken to England and Spain. Samoset introduced Squanto to the Pilgrims. Squanto knew English. He taught the Pilgrims about the New World.

After their first year, the Pilgrims celebrated a day of thanksgiving. They invited their Indian friends to eat together. They also played games together. They thanked God for all His blessings.

Today visitors can walk through a model of an early Pilgrim village.

Why did the Pilgrims move to the New World?

Living in the Americas

Long before Columbus discovered the Americas, people already lived there. How did those people get there? After the tower of Babel, people spread all over the world. Some traveled far across Asia. Most historians think people crossed the Bering Strait, the narrow strip of water between Russia and Alaska. From there the people went and filled all of the Americas.

The Olmecs were the first people in the Americas who built cities. They carved huge stone heads. They studied the stars and their movements. The Olmec **culture**, or way of life, showed much knowledge. Historians think the Olmecs were the first people to use rubber.

After the Olmecs, many other Indian groups lived in the Americas. Historians have found pyramids and carvings in Central and South America. They have also found huge mounds of dirt in North America. Indians built and used

A painting of John Eliot sharing God's Word with the Indians, painted in the 1800s

these mounds for their religion.

People of long ago had the ability to do many things. Indians knew the best ways to grow food. They planted corn, beans, squash, and potatoes. The Indians grew these before the rest of the world knew about them. Now people everywhere eat them. Christians should not be surprised that Indians built grand cities and were skilled farmers. God blessed man with the ability to rule over creation (Genesis 1:26–29).

Solving Problems

When the first colonists arrived in North America, the Indians taught them how to survive. The Indians had things the colonists wanted. The colonists had things the Indians wanted. They bartered with each other. **Barter** means to trade goods for other goods.

Some of the colonists wanted to teach the Indians to become Christians. A man named John Eliot *translated* the Bible for them. He wrote down what the Bible means in their Indian language. He also founded towns where the Indians could live as a Christian community. The Indians learned to read and write there. Eliot wanted them to study the Bible.

The Indians and the Europeans thought differently about some things. This caused problems. For example, Indians thought no one could own a piece of land forever. If an Indian bought land, he bought the right to use it only for a time. But a European bought land to own it for as long as he lived. He believed land was free if nobody claimed it. A European also believed that if he farmed or built on the land, it became his. Such misunderstandings led to fighting.

Jesus said we are to love others as we love ourselves. Sadness and suffering happen when this commandment is broken. The commandment was broken when the colonists mistreated the Indians and other people.

The meetinghouse was used for church services and other meetings.

The colonists brought some food and supplies from England. They also hunted, fished, gathered berries and nuts, and grew their own food.

The colonists made glass and worked with metals.

Houses were made from logs and had straw roofs. There was one big room for sleeping, cooking, eating, and working.

Many people from Europe and Africa came to North America. But many did not have money to pay for the trip. So they came as indentured servants. An *indentured servant* paid with work instead of money. For a time he would work for a master. After the servant worked enough to pay his debt, or the money he owed, he was free.

Amos Fortune

What: slave and businessman
When: 1710–1801
Where: Africa and New England

As a boy, Amos Fortune was captured and sold into slavery. He learned a trade. He also became a Christian. At the age of sixty, he bought his freedom. He did well in business and bought the freedom of other slaves. He also started a school.

As time passed, freedom changed for some people in America. Black people were not allowed to do the same things others could. Black people could not own weapons. They could not take people who had wronged them to court. Later, black people were made slaves for life because of the color of their skin. Making people slaves because of the color of their skin is a sin (Matthew 7:12 and 22:39). All sins have bad results. Americans would not escape the bad results of this sin.

How do most historians think people got to the Americas?

14

The Puritans

More people from England came to the New World. A group called the Puritans came soon after the Pilgrims. The Puritans did not agree with the Church of England. Many Puritans traveled to North America. They wanted to worship God in the way they thought was right. They called their settlement the **Massachusetts Bay Colony**.

The Puritans wanted a special culture. They wanted to give God honor in everything. To serve God, everyone needed to read the Bible and pray. Government, business, and art must glorify God too. The Puritans said only people who truly believed should be church members.

The Puritans discussing their government

The Puritans thought covenants were important. In the Bible God set up a **covenant**, or agreement, with Israel. God promised to bless Israel if they obeyed His law. If they disobeyed, God would punish Israel. The Puritans believed God had a covenant with them too. God would bless the Puritans if they obeyed Him. If they disobeyed, God would judge them. The Puritans knew that covenants cannot make someone God's child. A person becomes a Christian only through faith in Jesus.

The Puritans' colony grew quickly. It spread and formed new settlements dedicated to serving God.

This is a hand-colored woodcut of an 1800s drawing. It shows a 1620s Pilgrim church service.

What two groups of people traveled to the New World?

Examining Sources

Historians study items that have survived from the past. These items are called primary sources. **Primary sources** are written or made by people who were there when the event happened. The Mayflower Compact is a primary source. It was written by people who were there when it was made.

Historians also study secondary sources. **Secondary sources** are made by people who study a primary source. Secondary sources are made after an event happens. The *Mayflower II* is an example of a secondary source. It is a full-scale model of the *Mayflower*. The builders used primary sources to make the model. People can go to the Plimoth Plantation in Massachusetts to see the *Mayflower II*. It was built about 300 years after the original *Mayflower* sailed across the Atlantic.

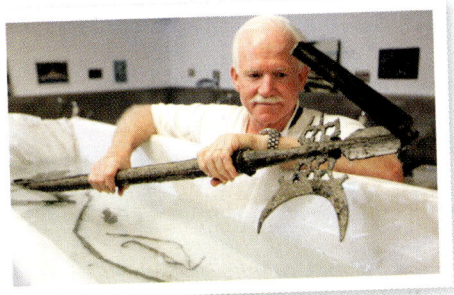

Primary or secondary source?

Primary or secondary source?

Primary Source	Secondary Source
letters written by Ben Franklin	encyclopedia entry about Ben Franklin
Columbus's log of his voyage	article written using Columbus's log
arrowhead uncovered at Jamestown	arrowhead drawing created in the 1900s

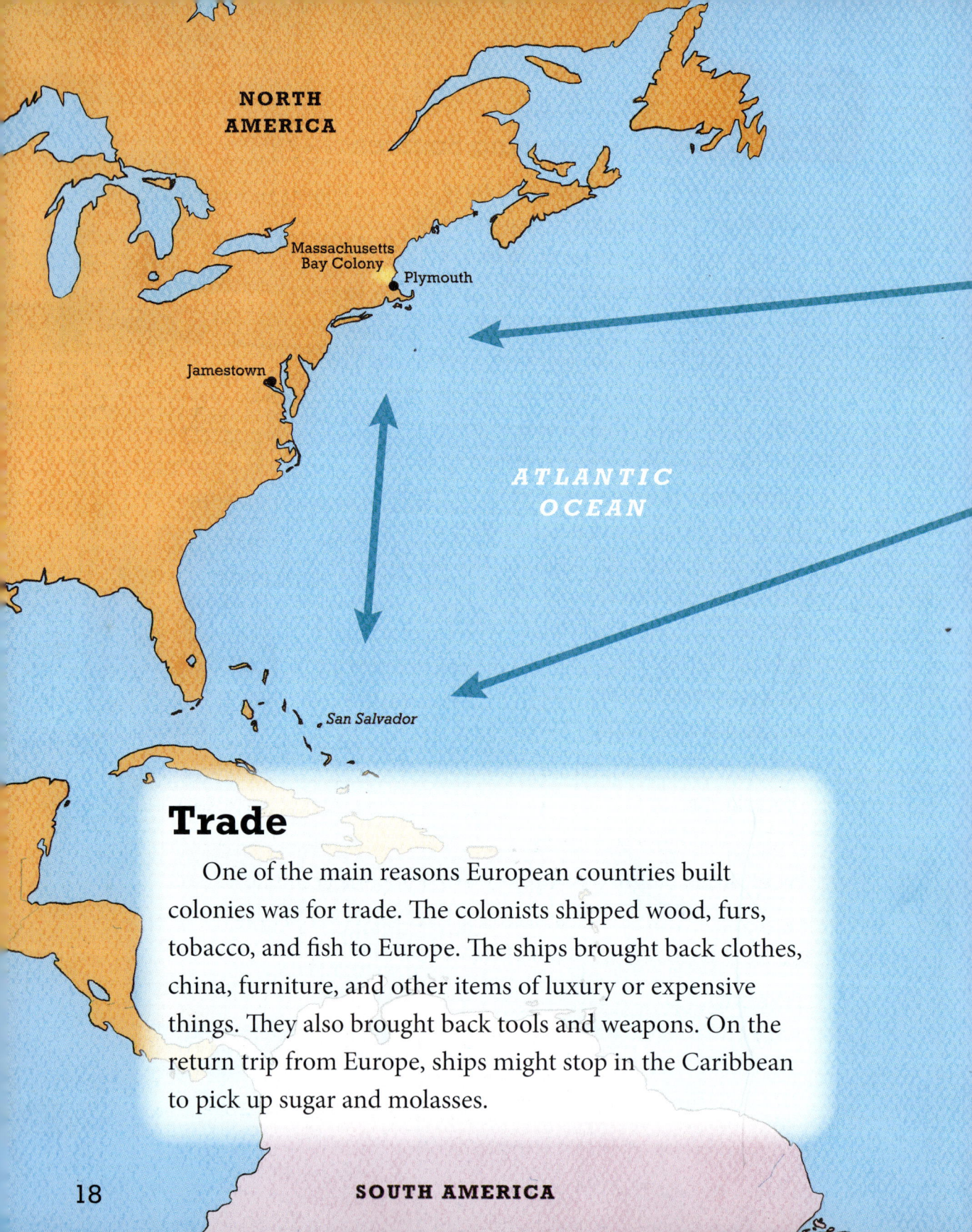

Trade

One of the main reasons European countries built colonies was for trade. The colonists shipped wood, furs, tobacco, and fish to Europe. The ships brought back clothes, china, furniture, and other items of luxury or expensive things. They also brought back tools and weapons. On the return trip from Europe, ships might stop in the Caribbean to pick up sugar and molasses.

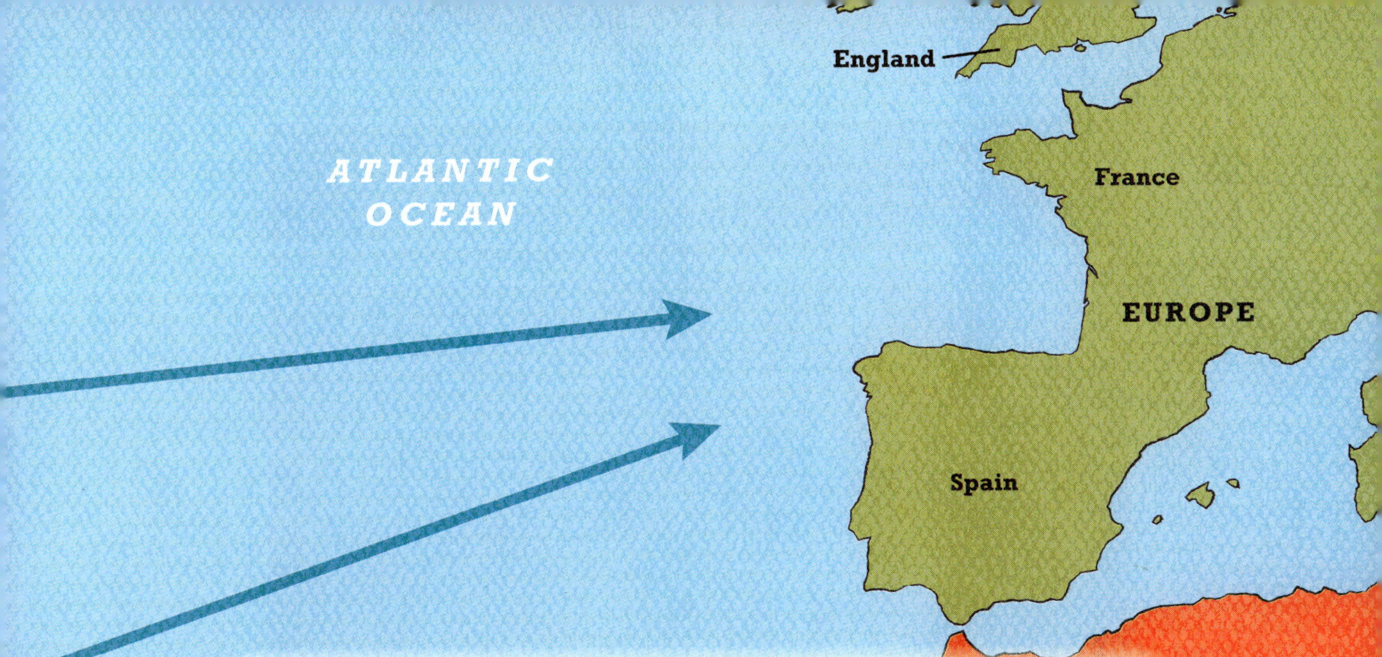

ATLANTIC
OCEAN

England

France

EUROPE

Spain

Sadly, Europeans and colonists also traded people. These people were sent to **plantations**, or large farms. Plantations needed many workers to grow sugarcane, coffee, tobacco, and cotton. Plantation owners bought workers from Africa. The Africans were packed tightly in ships. Then the long voyage began to the Caribbean and the colonies. Many died on the voyage. Many died as slaves in the Americas.

Some Christians thought it was wrong to own Christians as slaves. Most Africans were not Christians at this time, so some Christians believed it was not wrong to own African slaves. Jesus taught His followers that anyone could be a neighbor. Christians should not have enslaved people. Christians should have loved them as neighbors.

What was one of the main reasons Europe built colonies?

Preaching the truth of God's Word, George Whitefield (1714–1770) traveled throughout the colonies. Painting by John Collet (1725–1780).

The Great Awakening

In time the struggling colonies in North America grew. England and Scotland united as Britain, and more colonists traveled to the New World. Towns and cities were built. Trade made some colonists rich. The Puritans believed God blessed hard work with wealth. But some people became too interested in trade and wealth. They no longer wanted to talk with each other about God or worship Him. Fewer people said they knew Jesus as their Savior.

The Puritans said only Christians should be members of Puritan churches. But many of the Puritans' children were not Christians. If they grew up and stopped coming to church, the way of life in that town would no longer honor God.

The pastors knew that keeping people in church was important. Many pastors changed the rules for baptizing children. Parents did not have to be born-again Christians to have their children baptized. The parents simply needed to have been baptized as children themselves. In time many people who attended church, and even some of the pastors, were not true Christians.

Jonathan Edwards

At this time in the history of the colonies, God did something special. He sent a revival. A **revival** is when God works and many people come to know Him. God used preachers who knew Him to spread the revival. It spread over all the colonies.

Two preachers became famous during the revival. Jonathan Edwards was a pastor from the colony of Massachusetts. He preached of salvation through Christ. People who heard the message began to change. They began to love God and others more. God also used the preacher George Whitefield. He traveled north and south throughout the colonies. Many people turned to Christ. This return to true religion was known as the **Great Awakening**.

George Whitefield

The French and Indian War

After the Great Awakening, the colonists faced a new problem. France claimed all land north and west of the British colonies. However, the British colonists continued to move west. These colonists believed the land in the west belonged to Britain.

The French built forts and made treaties with the Indians. The French would not give land in North America to the British. The governor of the colony of Virginia sent a young George Washington to talk to the French. Washington told the French that their forts were on British land. He said they must leave. But the French refused to listen to Washington, and fighting began.

At first the French won many battles. But the British had a plan to win the most important battle. Both sides used rivers to ship supplies. The French mainly used the Saint Lawrence River. If the British could block it, the French could not get supplies. The British plan worked, and Britain won the war.

Winning the war did not solve the colonists' problems. The British gained land. But the British government decided that the colonists in North America could not move west. Indians and fur trappers would keep the land. The colonists were angry. They fought the war so they could move west. The colonists began to think of themselves as Americans instead of British.

Paying for the war created another problem. The British government spent much money on the war. They thought the colonists should pay taxes to help repay the cost. Britain said the taxes were fair because it fought to help the Americans. But the Americans did not think the taxes were fair. First, the Americans had done most of the fighting and fort building. Second, the Americans did not elect lawmakers to the British government. If Americans had to pay taxes, they should be a part of making the laws.

The Stamp Act required the colonies' newspapers to be printed on paper with tax stamps.

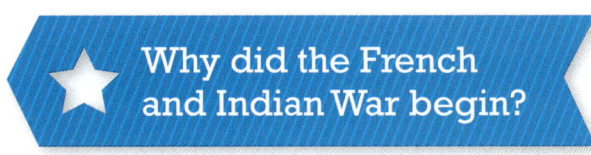

Why did the French and Indian War begin?

The Revolutionary War

The American leaders thought carefully about how a government should work. They believed people should not rebel against it. But when a government mistreated the people instead of protecting them, it rebelled against God's laws. If some parts of government mistreated the people, the other parts of government should help the people.

Many Americans felt that the British government was mistreating them. It made them pay taxes without letting Americans help write the laws for those taxes. The Americans wanted to choose American leaders who would help make the British laws. These leaders would be representatives for America. A **representative** is someone who people choose to act or speak for them.

The Americans also did not like that British soldiers were in American cities and homes. The soldiers were there to make sure the Americans obeyed the British government.

Minutemen fought in the Revolutionary War. These Americans were ready to defend their homes and towns in a minute.

In 1774, representatives from twelve of the colonies met as the First Continental Congress. They sent the British king a petition, or request. They asked him to fix the wrongs against them.

The petition did not help. The king said that the colonists must obey. Near the city of Boston, colonists gathered guns. If the king sent an army, there might be a war.

A British general told his soldiers to take the colonists' guns away. He sent soldiers to arrest the colonists' leaders. The British soldiers wanted to surprise the colonists. But Paul Revere and two other men warned the colonists that the British were coming. The Americans met the British soldiers at Lexington and Concord, Massachusetts. No one knows which side fired the first shot.

The British are giving up at Yorktown. Painted by John Trumbull in the early 1800s.

The Revolutionary War (or War for Independence) began with battles at Lexington and Concord. Americans from all the colonies joined to fight the British. George Washington commanded the Continental Army.

At first the British had great successes. But the colonists did not give up. They defeated the British in many battles. The Americans finally won the war at the battle of Yorktown. In 1783, the Americans and the British signed a peace treaty, or agreement. The war was over. America was now independent from Britain.

The Revolutionary War brought many changes. The most important change was America's independence. But not all changes from the war were good. The work of pastors became hard. New freedoms made people less willing to follow God, pastors, or churches. People still used religious language, but they cared more about being good Americans than being Christians. People believed living *moral*, or well-behaved, lives was enough. Some popular men who had supported the war did not believe that the Bible was God's Word. For many, Jesus was only a good moral example, not a Savior.

The Americans soon started a government. But it was weak. People's desire to serve God was also weak. But by God's grace, all this would change.

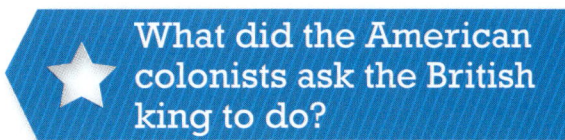

What did the American colonists ask the British king to do?

2 The Constitution

Focus
The American Republic is built on the Constitution's plan for a national government.

Working Together

America was now a free nation. It faced many changes. The American colonies were now called states. They were no longer colonies because Britain did not own them anymore. After the Revolutionary War, each state set up its own government.

America had thirteen states. Each state was like a small country. The states needed to find a way to work together. But no state wanted to give up too much freedom as it worked with the other states.

The states agreed to work together. They made a set of laws called the **Articles of Confederation**. It set up a national government for all thirteen states. But the states were given many rights. The states chose how much to tax their people. The states decided if their men had to join an army.

The Articles of Confederation

The national government could ask the states for money or soldiers. But the states could choose to agree or not. The Articles even let states make treaties with other countries.

There were other changes for America. Americans were moving west. This caused problems because no one knew who owned what lands. Sometimes two or more states claimed the same land. In the end, the states gave the western lands to the national government.

Western Lands

There were fourteen different kinds of money in the early United States.

Problems Arise

As the states tried to work together, the new country faced many problems. The national government was weak. Its leaders were not always wise. And it owed a lot of money because of the Revolutionary War. Money that is owed is called *debt*.

State governments faced these same problems. Many state governments had leaders who did not make good choices. People often thought character and education did not matter during elections. They thought anyone could serve as a leader. Some leaders made selfish or foolish laws. Some states also made their people pay higher taxes to pay off state debts. Soldiers who returned home to farm found it hard to pay their bills. Taxes were too high.

In Massachusetts, **Daniel Shays** led a rebellion against the state. He used to be a soldier. Now he was a farmer at home. He was afraid he would lose his farm because he could not pay his bills. About two thousand men joined him. They attacked a courthouse and a weapons storehouse. The state sent soldiers and they stopped Shays' Rebellion.

Shays' Rebellion worried people. They feared that a mob, or crowd, might fight and try to rule the states. Some asked if the Articles of Confederation was strong enough to hold the country together. The national government needed to be able to stop people who broke the law.

George Washington

Twelve states sent delegates to a convention, or meeting, in Philadelphia. A **delegate** is a person who represents a group of people. The delegates' task was to make the Articles of Confederation stronger and better. The delegates decided to write the United States Constitution. One of the delegates was George Washington. He wanted to serve his country. He did not seek power. This made people more hopeful. Most Americans trusted Washington to make wise choices. When the delegates chose Washington as their leader, many people believed that the convention would solve the nation's problems.

What were some problems the new country faced?

Mount Vernon, Washington's home, was used at times for government meetings.

Constitutional Convention

The state delegates gathered at the Constitutional Convention. They met in the summer of **1787** in **Philadelphia**. The delegates had big goals. Many of these men had helped write their state constitutions. They knew what laws worked well.

Americans feared rule by one man or by a mob. The delegates needed to design a good government. They wanted a balanced type of government: a republic. In a **republic**, representatives run the government. People in a republic take part in government through the representatives they elect.

A republic needs citizens of virtue. A person of virtue is wise, good, fair, and moral. Voters usually choose people like themselves when they elect their rulers. If the people have virtue, usually the leaders they choose do too.

Designing a good republic would not be easy. The delegates planned to work hard. But often they did not agree on the best plan.

Plans for a New Government

James Madison was the delegate with the most plans. He wanted to make the government work better for everyone. He studied law and government. He had served in both state and national government. He had much knowledge.

Madison went to the Constitutional Convention with plans for a new government. His ideas formed the basis of the United States Constitution. The other delegates liked some of his ideas. But they did not agree with all of them.

Branches of National Government

The delegates agreed with one of Madison's plans. He wanted to split the new government into three branches, or parts. This plan made sure no part was too powerful. The **executive branch** was the president. The **judicial branch** was the Supreme Court. It was made up of judges. The **legislative branch** was Congress. It was made up of representatives from the states. Each branch had a different job to do.

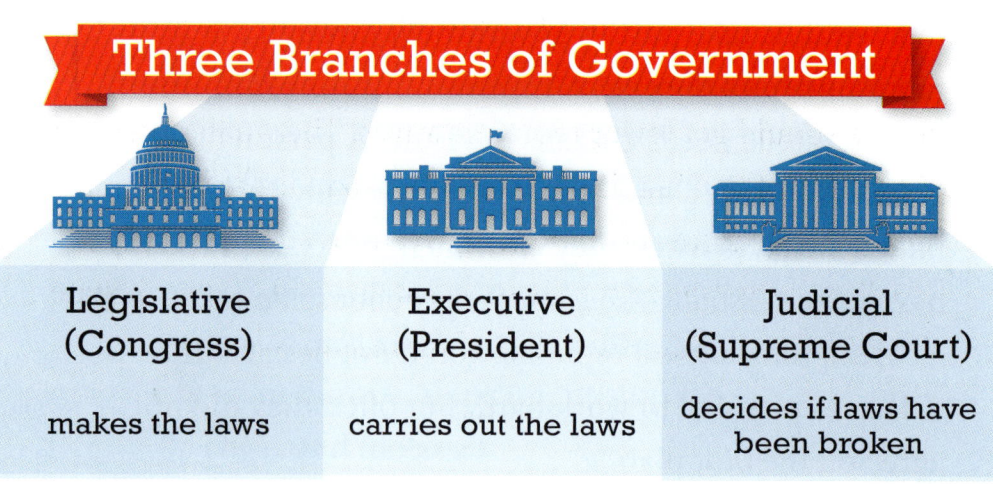

Two Plans for Congress

Madison's Plan

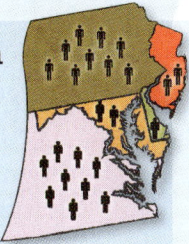

Representation in Congress based on population

The Small States' Plan

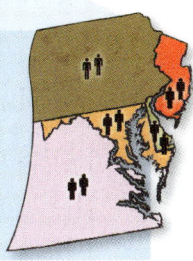

Representation in Congress equal for each state

Today the branches of government can check, or limit, each other's work. The president checks Congress. This group makes bills. The president must sign their bills before they become laws. He and the Congress check the Supreme Court. The president chooses the Supreme Court judges. Then Congress must approve, or accept, them. The Supreme Court checks the other two branches. It decides whether their laws and actions obey the Constitution.

The Articles of Confederation gave each state one vote in Congress. But Madison thought that states with more people should get more representatives. States with fewer people should get fewer representatives. The small states did not like this idea. If the large states had more votes, they could control the national government. No one would listen to the small states. The small states said that each state should have the same number of representatives.

The Great Compromise

House of Representatives
(based on population)

Senate
(same number from each state)

Compromise

One delegate came up with a compromise. A **compromise** is an agreement that is not exactly what either side wants but something both sides can agree to. The **Great Compromise** divided Congress into two groups. One group was the House of Representatives. The other group was the Senate. In the House, each state would have a certain number of representatives. This number would depend on how large or small that state was. In the Senate, each state would have two representatives. Both the large states and the small states accepted this plan. Both got what they wanted.

However, even after solving this problem, the delegates had other arguments.

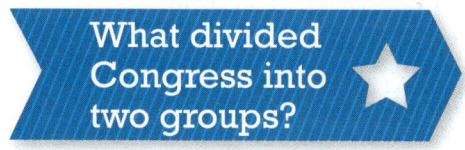

What divided Congress into two groups?

Slavery

The delegates spent a lot of time talking about slavery. Most had strong opinions. Americans had fought to be free from Britain. But many of them did not want to free their slaves. Some people said that slavery should end. Others thought that ending slavery would harm America.

Many Americans made money because of slavery. In the South, most slaves worked on plantations. They grew rice, tobacco, and cotton. Some owners said they needed more slaves.

George Mason from Virginia was worried about slavery in America. He told the delegates that they would "bring the judgment of heaven on a Country." But South Carolina and Georgia said they would only join a country that allowed people to buy slaves from Africa. The delegates did not want to argue about this now. They decided that Congress could decide what to do with slavery later on.

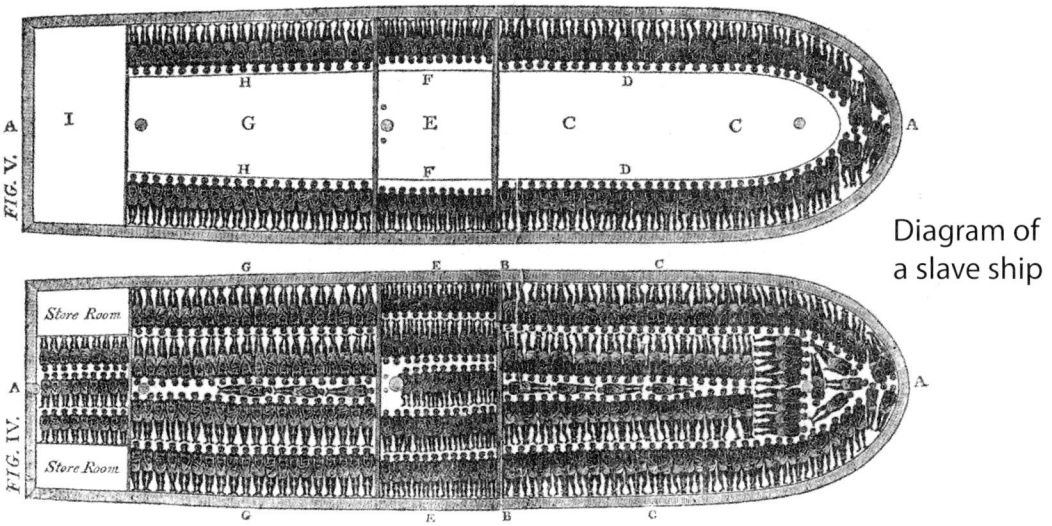

Diagram of a slave ship

The delegates did make two decisions about slavery. The first had to do with counting slaves. Only some would count toward representation in Congress and toward taxes. The second decision was about slaves who ran away. It said that these slaves must be returned to their masters.

These choices about slavery had an effect on America for many years. Many northerners wanted to end slavery. Many southerners wanted to keep slavery. All this disagreement helped cause the Civil War many years later and proved Mason's warning to be true.

Trade

Trade was important in America. States traded goods with each other and other countries. State governments made money from tariffs. A **tariff** is a tax on goods coming into a country. Goods that come into a country are called **imports**. Goods that leave a country are called **exports**. At this time each state had its own rules about trade. A state decided how much its tariffs should be on goods from other states or countries.

	imports	goods that come into a country
	exports	goods that leave a country

Ships at a harbor carrying imports and exports

People from the North and the South had different opinions about tariffs. The North had many factories. So it had more *manufacturing*, or the making of goods. Because the North produced many goods, it did not need as many imports as the South. Northerners wanted high tariffs on imports. This would make people want to buy northern goods rather than expensive imports.

The South had few factories. It did not have as many goods as the North. The South needed imports. This made southerners want low tariffs on imports.

The delegates thought American trade would be stronger if all the states obeyed the same rules. The national government would decide the tariff for trade with other countries. Also, no state could put a tariff on another state's goods.

Even though the delegates did not always agree, they kept working. They wrote the Constitution by the end of the summer.

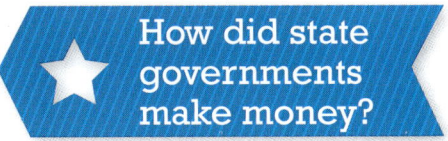

How did state governments make money?

Purposes of the Constitution

A document as important as the United States Constitution needs a good **preamble**, or introduction. The Constitution starts with the words "We the people." It lists the six major purposes for the Constitution.

Form a more perfect union. The union of states made by the Articles of Confederation needed to be stronger. The Constitution set up a strong national government. But the national government was limited by the rights of the states and the people. So far, this union has lasted.

Establish justice. The Bible says that this is the main responsibility of any government. To establish justice means that a government helps people to act rightly toward each other. A government does this by rewarding good behavior and punishing bad behavior.

Signing of the Constitution by Howard Chandler Christy (1873–1952)

Insure domestic tranquility. The Articles of Confederation could not solve problems inside America. This resulted in Shays' Rebellion. The founders, or the leaders who wrote the Constitution, hoped for peace, or tranquility, among all American citizens in America.

Provide for the common defense. The founders had learned from their experience in the Revolutionary War. They wanted the national government to defend the nation from other countries if America faced another war.

Promote the general welfare. People live in communities and nations. The Constitution is not supposed to help only some individuals or certain groups of people. The Constitution is to benefit everyone.

Secure the blessings of liberty. The founders fought for liberty, or freedom, in the Revolutionary War. But freedom comes with laws. The Constitution is the law that makes sure Americans keep their liberty.

Understanding and Memorizing the Preamble

- Read the Preamble in the Resource Treasury.
- Discuss the meaning of the Preamble with the teacher.
- Memorize a new phrase of the Preamble each day.

Constitution Completed

The delegates took four months to write the Constitution. Many times they did not agree with each other. After much talk and compromise, they finally finished the plan for America's new government.

Washington's chair

Benjamin Franklin, a delegate from Pennsylvania, helped write the Constitution. Toward the end of the Convention, he wrote a speech. First, he said that he did not agree with every part of the Constitution. But he added,

Close-up view of chair

"The older I grow, the more [likely] I am to doubt my own judgment and to pay more respect to the judgment of others." Franklin said that all the delegates should vote for the Constitution. He thought it was the best constitution they could make.

Most of the delegates agreed with Franklin. They signed the Constitution. Franklin had often looked at George Washington's chair. It had half of a sun carved on it. Franklin often looked at that sun during the times the delegates argued over decisions. He wondered whether it was a rising sun or a setting sun.

Franklin told the delegates, "Now at length I have the happiness to know that it is a rising and not a setting sun." But the Constitution needed more work to become law.

Federalists & Anti-Federalists

The Constitution did not become law as soon as the delegates signed it. The states first needed to approve it. If nine of thirteen states approved, it would become law.

Not all Americans liked the Constitution. People who liked the Constitution were called **Federalists**. They thought the states should accept it. People who did not like it were called **Anti-Federalists**. They thought the Constitution was a bad idea. They believed it took away too much power from the people and the states. The Anti-Federalists wanted a statement, or bill, of rights to protect their freedom.

The Federalists thought that a bill of rights was not needed. The Constitution listed the national government's powers. The people and the states had all other powers.

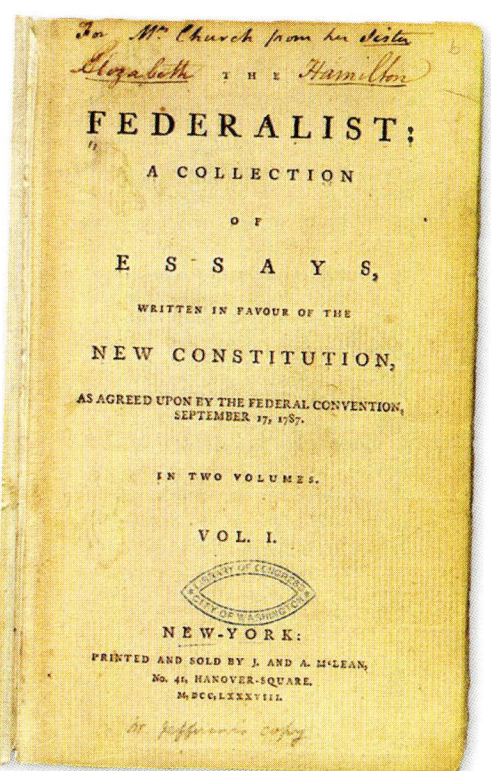

Title page of the first printing of *The Federalist Papers*, which encouraged people to support the Constitution

Photograph of the Independence Hall tower, taken in 2009. Delegates wrote the Constitution here in 1787.

The Anti-Federalists wanted written limits on the national government. These would tell what the national government could not do. Anti-Federalists thought it might take more freedoms from the people and the states. The Americans had fought the Revolutionary War to win freedom from a powerful government.

Many Americans agreed that the Constitution needed a bill of rights. Even though they trusted the Constitution, they knew it set up a strong government. Americans wanted to protect their freedoms from that government.

How many states needed to approve the Constitution to make it the law?

Religious Freedom

Many people worried about the Constitution. Some heroes of the Revolutionary War were Anti-Federalists. Baptists in Virginia also wanted a bill of rights. They wanted to have equal freedom with other people. The Baptists had often been treated badly. They wanted to protect their freedom of religion.

James Madison needed help to get Virginia to **ratify**, or approve, the Constitution. Some historians believe he talked with the Baptists. Madison likely told them that once a new Congress met, he would support a bill of rights. The bill would protect religious freedom.

Madison's plan worked. With support from the Baptists, Virginia soon voted in favor of the Constitution. When Madison went to Congress, he introduced the Bill of Rights.

Isaac Backus

What: pastor
When: 1724–1806
Where: Massachusetts

Isaac Backus was a Baptist pastor for many years. He wrote and spoke to encourage people to believe the Bible. He encouraged other Baptists who were often treated unfairly. Backus wanted Baptists to vote for the Constitution.

Approval of the States

While Virginia was deciding what to do, other states voted in favor of the Constitution. Delaware was the first. Within half a year, eight states had ratified the Constitution.

One more state was needed. The Constitution could only become law if at least nine states approved it. Finally, New Hampshire became the ninth. The United States now had a new government.

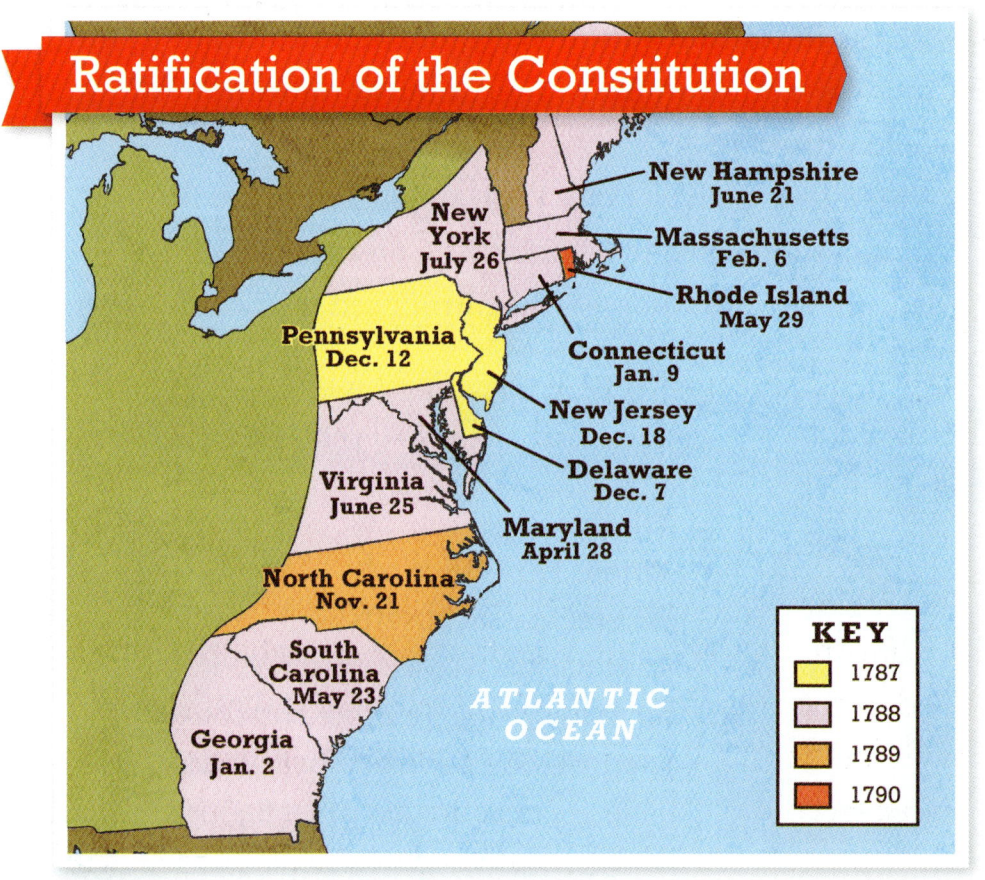

Four states did not sign the Constitution. Instead, they waited. Many people in Virginia and New York thought their states could survive as independent countries. North Carolina and Rhode Island were concerned about losing freedoms. However, in the end, all thirteen states approved the Constitution.

Strength of the Constitution

The United States Constitution has lasted longer than any other written constitution. Two major reasons explain its long life.

First, its authors were wise. Most of the founding fathers were well educated and had virtue. Many were not Christians, but all knew the Bible well. They also studied other governments. Since people often make bad choices, the founders designed a limited government. No part could easily tell another what to do. Each part limits the others.

Second, God gave grace to America. Without true religion and morals, a nation will struggle to survive. God blessed America with revivals that changed people to love God and others. This change led people to live moral lives. It made the nation secure and strong. Many nations have tried to copy the Constitution, but few have succeeded. Without the blessing of God, the Constitution is only words on paper.

> What did James Madison introduce in Congress?

3 Presidents & Precedents

Focus
As first president of the United States, George Washington set good precedents.

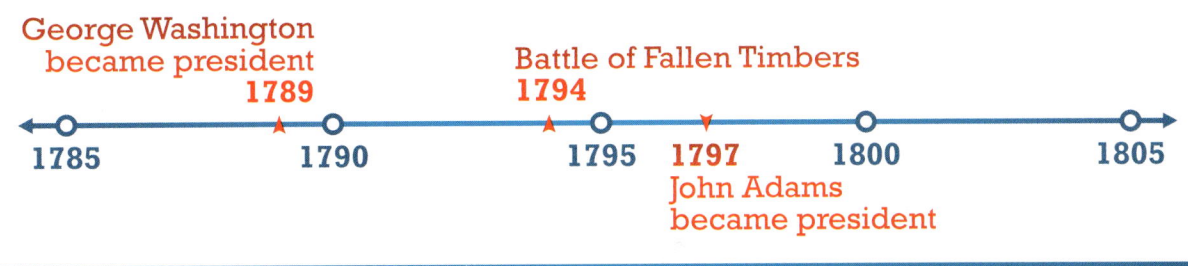

The First President

George Washington influenced, or had an effect on, the United States more than anyone else in his time. He helped the Americans win the Revolutionary War. He was part of the Constitutional Convention. There he helped form the new government. People trusted it because of him. Later he became the first American president. He set **precedents**, or examples, for all other presidents.

Washington as a Farmer at Mount Vernon,
painted by Junius Brutus Stearns, 1851

People trusted George Washington. Sometimes a general who wins a war wants power. He might make himself leader of the nation. Washington was a general who helped win a war. But he did not make himself leader of the United States. Instead, he went home. He wanted to run his plantation as a normal citizen.

Some were afraid that having a president would be like having a king. Washington did not want to be a king. He was not sure he wanted to be president. But he did want to serve his country. He believed good character was important for good government. Washington wanted to set a good example for the future.

Electoral College

Many Americans wanted George Washington to be president. Most Americans who could vote wanted him to lead the new country.

The founders of America wanted the people to help choose the president. But the people might choose someone just because he was popular. Being popular does not make a person a good president. A president must have the character to do the right things. He must know how to make good choices.

So the founders decided to create the **Electoral College**. This group was made up of electors, or people who represented each state. They would vote to choose the next president.

When the Electoral College voted, all the electors chose George Washington. He is the only president who was chosen by all the electors. They knew he had the character to make good choices.

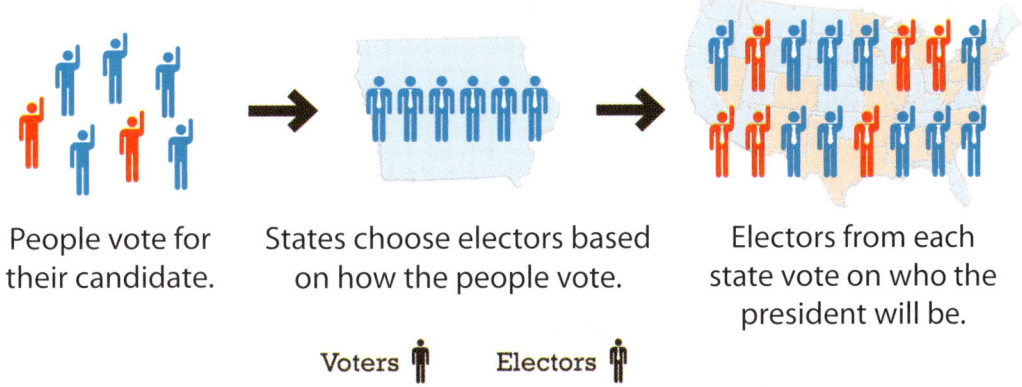

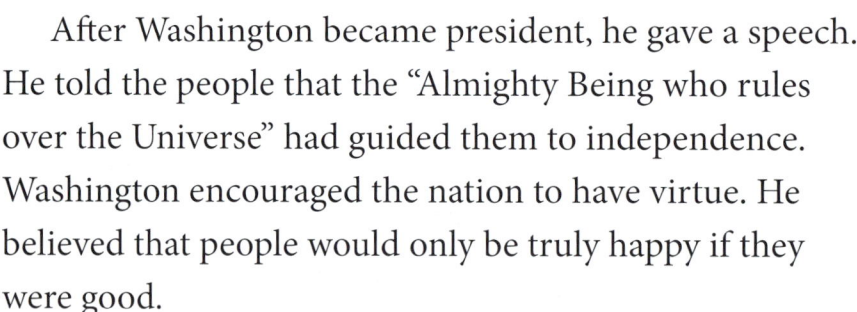

Voting then and now

After Washington became president, he gave a speech. He told the people that the "Almighty Being who rules over the Universe" had guided them to independence. Washington encouraged the nation to have virtue. He believed that people would only be truly happy if they were good.

How was George Washington elected as president?

Religion in Early America

Like Washington, the founders valued virtue. They wanted Americans to behave well. Some said that if America's leaders did not have virtue, the nation would fail. Good leaders need to care for others. They must not put themselves first. The people must do the same.

The founders tried to give good advice. But sometimes they did not. Some of them were Christians. But some founders thought the Bible did not matter. They thought it was enough for a person to want to do right. A few thought that Jesus was not God. Yet most believed the Bible was helpful.

John Adams

"Wisdom and knowledge, as well as virtue, diffused generally among the body of the people" is "necessary for the preservation of their rights and liberties."

This means if people want to keep their freedom, they must be wise and good.

Some founders believed that any religion was as good as another. They just wanted people to be moral. These founders did not like arguing about Christian teachings. They thought it did not matter if a nation's leaders were Christians. The founders wanted to allow a person to serve in the national government even if he did not believe in a religion.

This upset many people. They thought only Christians could be good leaders. Some states only allowed leaders whose religion was Christianity.

Outside and inside the Old Ship Church in Hingham, Massachusetts. Built in 1681, it served as a place of worship on Sundays and as a meetinghouse.

Camp Meeting of the Methodists in North America, painted by Jacques Gérard Milbert, 1819

Some people thought religion would disappear. One government leader, Thomas Jefferson, believed that people were changing. He thought they would give up religion. He did not think many young people would be Christians when they grew up.

But Jefferson was wrong. During the early 1800s, a revival took place. Many Americans became **Evangelical Christians**. They said that the Bible is the final authority. They taught that sin is people's biggest problem. They taught that people can be saved because Christ died and rose from the dead. They believed a person can be saved from sin if he trusts in Christ.

There were many groups of Evangelical Christians. Methodists and Baptists were both important groups in the revival. They spread into the West. Some western towns had no preacher. One man might preach for several towns. He could ride from town to town on a planned circuit, or route. These men were called **circuit-riding preachers**. Revival also happened in the East.

Many people heard the Bible and changed. They left their sin and trusted Christ. The revival proved Jefferson wrong. He thought people would not care for religion. But many Americans did care. During the 1800s, many Americans became Evangelical Christians.

Francis Asbury helped form the Methodist church in America. For over thirty years he rode from town to town and shared the gospel.

What was a circuit-riding preacher?

Washington's Cabinet

During this time of change, George Washington became president. He had much to do. The president leads the executive branch of the government. This branch makes sure that the country runs according to the law. One person cannot do this job alone. The president chooses people for help and advice. They are the **cabinet**.

George Washington chose four men he trusted and knew well. The men did not always agree. But Washington wanted the best men even if they did not agree.

Washington gave each of the men a job. **Thomas Jefferson** became the secretary of state. He helped America and other nations get along. **Alexander Hamilton** became the secretary of the treasury. He took care of all the nation's money. Henry Knox became the secretary of war. He was in charge of the United States military. Edmund Randolph became the attorney general. He was in charge of making people obey the national law.

These men formed Washington's cabinet. He trusted them to give him good help.

Sometimes Washington had to choose whose advice to listen to. Two men on his cabinet did not agree about the national government. Alexander Hamilton thought that having a strong government in charge was good. It helped people. But Thomas Jefferson said less government was better.

Washington and His Cabinet

George Washington
President
Washington set precedents in choosing his cabinet.

Thomas Jefferson
Secretary of State
He helped America and other nations get along.

Alexander Hamilton
Secretary of the Treasury
He was in charge of all of the nation's money.

Henry Knox
Secretary of War
He was in charge of the US military.

Edmund Randolph
Attorney General
He was in charge of making people obey the national law.

Washington needed advice on starting a national bank. Jefferson said it was a bad idea. He did not want people to borrow money from a bank. Some people might not be able to pay the bank back. Also, banks were in cities. Jefferson thought people should live on farms, not in cities. Hamilton thought a national bank was a good idea. The bank could print money for the nation. The government could keep its money safe in the bank. If the government or businesses needed money, they could borrow from the bank.

Washington needed more advice. Did the Constitution allow Congress to start a national bank? Jefferson said no. The Constitution did not clearly say so. So Jefferson believed starting the bank was not lawful. But Hamilton said yes. The Constitution said the government should do anything necessary and proper to do its job. Hamilton thought starting a national bank was the right thing to do.

In the end, Washington agreed with Hamilton and set up a national bank. But Hamilton and Jefferson kept on disagreeing. Some Americans took sides. But most Americans loved Washington as president. They agreed with his choices.

First Bank of the United States, in Philadelphia

What are the people who help the president called?

Planning a Budget

The national government needs a budget. A **budget** is a plan for spending and saving money. A budget shows the amount of *income*. This is the money that comes in. The nation's income comes from taxes. A person's income comes from his job. A budget also shows the amount of *expenses*. This is money used for goods and services. Using money for goods and services is called *spending*. Keeping a budget can help save money. Then this money can go to *savings*. This is money that is not spent.

Western Settlement

Banks, cities, and trade were not the only concerns of the government. It also had to take care of people moving west. George Washington wanted this to happen in a slow and planned way. Many Indians still lived in the West. They did not like many new people moving into their lands. Washington did not want to wrong the Indians.

The Indians still controlled much land in the West. So the national government separated the other land into even parts. People were allowed to buy only large sections of land. Washington wanted wealthy and virtuous people to start towns with schools.

But American settlers did not follow the government's plan. They did not think that the government could sell land that nobody lived on. If nobody was using the land, it should be free to take. But when settlers looked for land, the Indians often told them it was being used. The Indians used the land for hunting, even if they did not live there. American settlers kept moving farther west. The Indians were not happy. Many Indians wanted to fight for their land.

Washington and Henry Knox did not want to push the Indians out of their land. Knox thought the Indians had a right to the land. They lived there first. But as settlers moved west, they fought with the Indians.

Henry Knox

"The Indians being the prior occupants possess the right of the soil."

The British still had men and forts in the Northwest. Like the Indians, the British did not want America to take more land. So the British traded weapons to the Indians.

Washington picked General **Anthony Wayne** to train an army. Wayne's army fought the British and the Indians. Wayne defeated the Indians at the **Battle of Fallen Timbers**.

The Road to Fallen Timbers, painted by H. Charles McBarron Jr., 1953

Wayne's victory brought many changes. After the Battle of Fallen Timbers, Washington sent John Jay to Britain. Jay told the British to leave American lands. The British agreed. America and Britain began to work together. At this time, America had problems with Spain. They argued about land in the South. Spain would not let Americans ship goods down the Mississippi River through the city of

New Orleans. Spain controlled this city. But when Britain and America stopped fighting, Spain settled its problems with America. Spain did not want to cause trouble. Britain and America might join armies and fight back.

Changes also happened in America. Settlers in the Northwest were happy with the national government. It had helped them. But settlers in the Southwest were not as happy. They kept fighting the Indians. The national government did not help the southwestern Americans. Instead, it told them to make peace with the Indians. It also told the settlers to stop taking Indian lands. This upset some Americans.

The national government had an effect on people's lives. Anthony Wayne's victory and the agreements with Great Britain and Spain changed how people lived. However, state and local governments had a bigger effect on people's lives.

The American Soldier, 1794, painted by H. Charles McBarron Jr., 1964

Types of Government			
National	president	Congress	courts
State	governor	legislature	courts
Local	mayor	city council	courts

The state government is like the national government. The national government has a president, Congress, and courts to govern the nation. A state government has a governor, a legislature, and courts to govern the state. A legislature is a group of representatives who pass laws. A local government has a mayor and courts. Many local governments have a city council. A local government governs a county or a city in a state.

When Americans moved west, they left behind their state and their local governments. The settlers moved to *territories*, land owned by a national government. There were no state or local governments in territories. Settlers had to govern their own communities. They had to work out how to get along with their neighbors on their own.

What problems did America have with Spain?

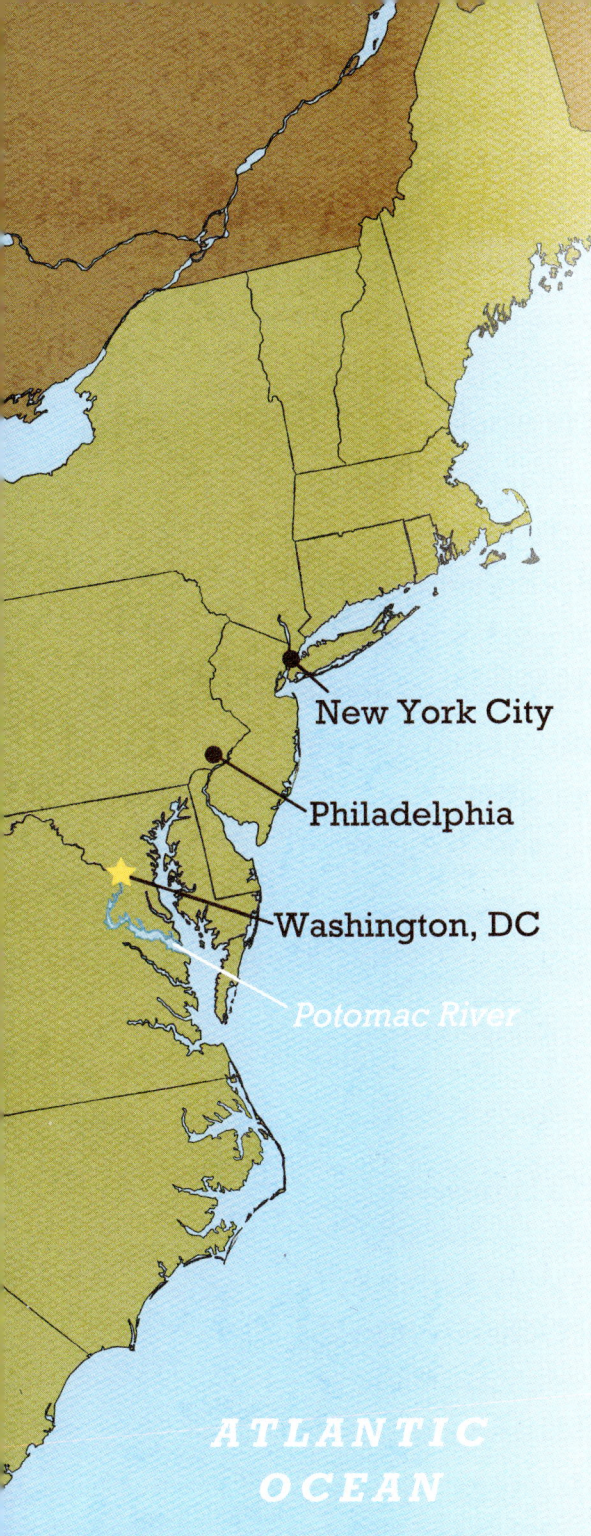

The Capital

The national government needed a capital for the United States. Where should the capital be built? The founders did not want the capital to be in a state. They gave Congress the power to plan an area for the capital. Congress would control the area.

New York City was the nation's capital when George Washington became president. But most Americans thought it should not stay there. America's leaders did not agree on where the capital should be. Hamilton liked New York City. Jefferson thought a place near the South would be better.

Hamilton and Jefferson also did not agree on the debt from the Revolutionary War. The war was expensive. Some states now owed a lot of money. Hamilton wanted the national government to pay the debts of all the states. But Jefferson thought each state should pay its own debt. Both men made a deal. The government would pay for the war debts for all the states. And the capital would be in the South. Both men got part of what they wanted.

Two states gave land for the capital. This land was next to the **Potomac River**. Now the nation needed to plan and build the capital city. Jefferson wanted a small city about the size of a college. But Washington wanted a large and grand city. He wanted a capital for a growing nation.

Benjamin Banneker

What: farmer, scientist, inventor
When: 1731–1806
Where: Maryland

Banneker was raised a farmer. He helped survey, or measure the area of, Washington, DC. He also wrote an almanac. He invented America's first working clock. He was always learning and working throughout his life.

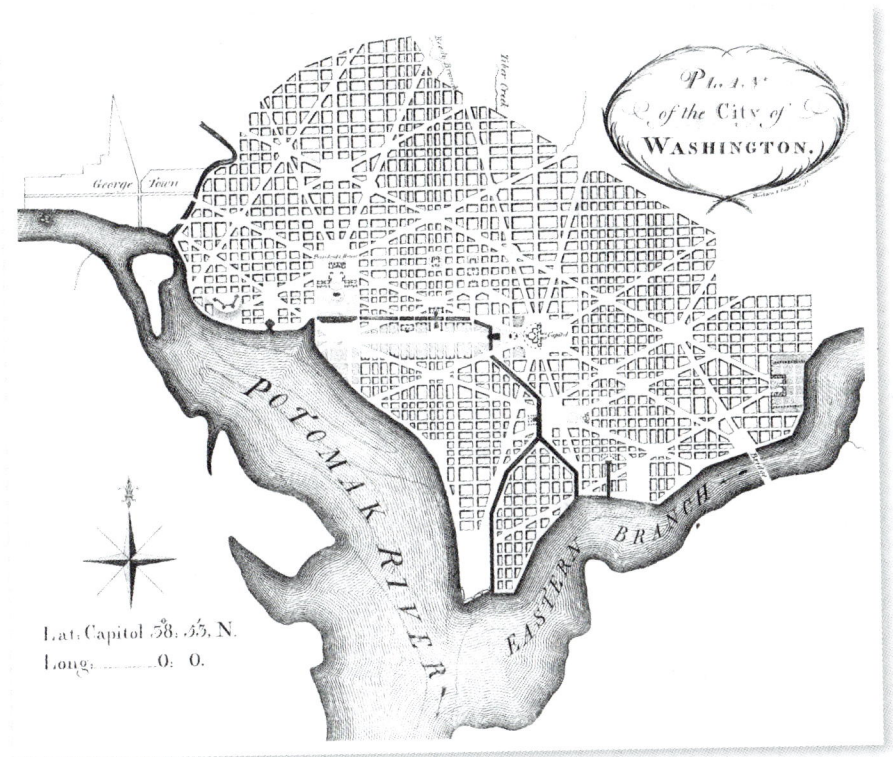

Washington asked Pierre L'Enfant to plan the city. L'Enfant set up the city with a grid of streets. He planned wide avenues leading to the president's house and the Capitol. He put aside special areas for colleges, monuments, and a national church building. L'Enfant planned a grand city known as the city of Washington. It was named after the first president. The city area was called the District of Columbia. It was named after the explorer Christopher Columbus. Today the capital's name is **Washington, DC**.

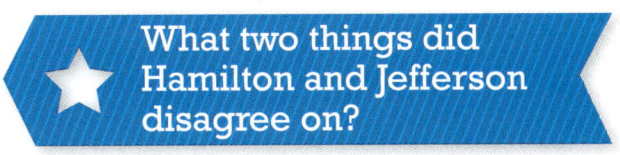

What two things did Hamilton and Jefferson disagree on?

Precedents of the President

George Washington knew he was setting precedents for future presidents. He took care with each precedent he set. As general, Washington's most important precedent was to let Congress command the army.

Washington wanted the people to respect the job of president. He was careful about the way he dressed and acted. For example, he always wore a dark suit.

Washington set another example. He took responsibility for the choices of the executive branch. Sometimes people argued about a decision. But he would make a decision and stick with it.

Washington had the authority to hire and fire workers in the executive branch. Some members of Congress wanted him to ask them before firing workers. Washington refused. This gave the president more power in the executive branch.

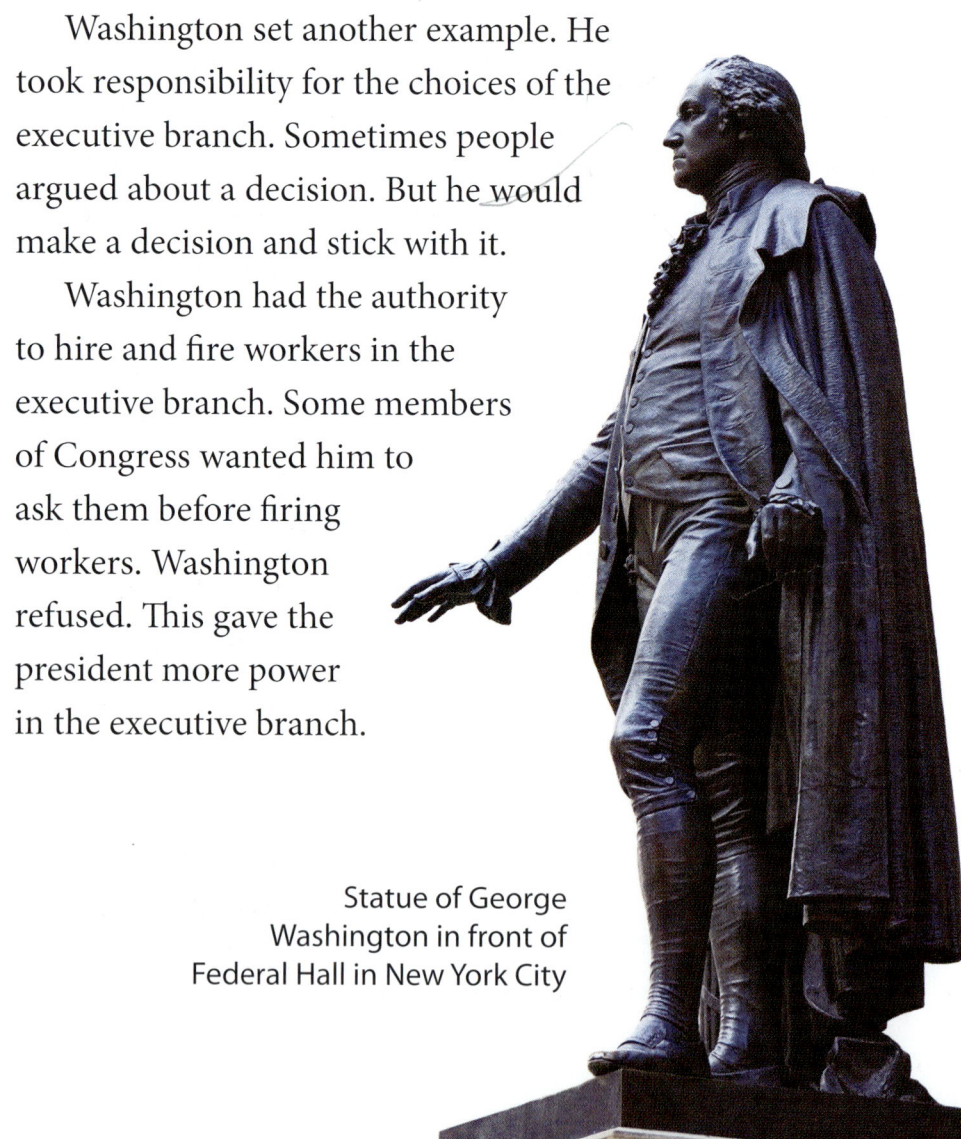

Statue of George Washington in front of Federal Hall in New York City

Washington left after two terms as president. A term lasts for four years. Many thought the president would serve for life. Serving for two terms was Washington's most important precedent when he was president. Other presidents did the same and served for only two terms. This example was followed into the 1900s.

Farewell Address

George Washington spoke to the nation before he left office. This speech was his farewell address. The speech explained why he was not continuing as president. Most of the speech was advice to the nation.

Washington wanted the nation to be united, or together. He told the people not to let differences separate them. He said what united them was greater than what might separate them. If the nation separated, it would hurt the people.

Washington's Farewell Address, 1796

 Washington worried that political parties were separating the nation. **Political parties** are groups of people who try to gain power in government. They weaken the power of the government. Washington warned that political parties would not look out for the good of the whole nation. They would put their own plans first. They would not always do what was best for all the people.

Washington said that a successful nation needed to be based on good morals. Its people should do what was right and moral.

 Washington closed his speech by warning against large debts. The nation might need to borrow money. He believed that debts should be paid off quickly. Washington also warned about making agreements with other nations. Some nations had different ideas from the United States. This might cause problems. He also said the United States should create good trading opportunities. But it should not make promises that would hurt the nation.

With his farewell address, Washington left the nation with wisdom for years to come.

As president, what was Washington's most important precedent?

John Adams

Not all Americans agreed on who to choose for a new president. Many people thought Thomas Jefferson would do a good job. But **John Adams** had served as vice president for eight years. He read about and studied government throughout his entire life. Adams even wrote books about how government should work.

Painting of President John Adams by Asher B. Durand

In 1796 electors voted for a new president. Three more voted for Adams than for Jefferson. Adams became the second president. He was the first to live in the new capital city.

Political Parties

President Adams had a new problem to deal with. When Washington was president, Americans had formed political parties. These groups did not agree with each other about politics, or matters of government. Washington had warned the people about political parties.

There were two main parties. The **Federalists** liked Alexander Hamilton's ideas. The Federalists wanted the United States to be powerful in banking and trading. People who lived in northern cities were usually Federalists. The **Democratic-Republicans** liked Thomas Jefferson's ideas. The Democratic-Republicans wanted the United States to be a nation of farmers. This party did not like wealth from banks and trade. The Democratic-Republicans believed too much wealth made people unequal. Wealth gave some people more power than others. Too much money could separate America into rich and poor people.

Like Washington, Adams did not want people to join political parties. The government should try to help everyone. It should help banks, trade, and farms. But most people still joined a political party. They joined the one they agreed with.

Adams soon had to prove he would not pick one side over another. America and France were not getting along. The Federalists thought America should fight France. They also supported Adams. The Democratic-Republicans did not support Adams. And they did not want war.

Adams wanted to do what was best for America. He did not want America to go to war. The Democratic-Republicans still did not like him. The Federalists were angry with him. Adams did not change his decision. He believed he did what was right.

Adams's Decision

Adams did not always make wise decisions. Newspapers started supporting political parties. The papers printed both true and false things about both parties. This included things about government officials from the parties. Adams thought these actions were wrong. He signed a law to make it illegal to attack government officials in print.

Thomas Jefferson and James Madison said this law disagreed with the Constitution. It states that everyone has a right to free speech. But this new law did not allow people to speak freely about the government. Many Americans did not like this law. The people knew Adams signed it. He became unpopular. The law lasted only until the end of his presidency.

Early 1800s printing press

John Adams stood on his beliefs, right or wrong. Some people did not agree with his beliefs. So he lost the presidential election of 1800. He also lost friends.

Adams's wife, Abigail, was his faithful friend for fifty-four years of marriage. By reading books, Abigail Adams taught herself about government and many other things.

Painting of Abigail Smith Adams by Gilbert Stuart, started in 1800 and finished in 1815

John Adams wrote his wife letters asking for advice. She gave him wise and educated advice. They loved and helped each other.

Both George Washington and John Adams served their country. They chose what they believed was best for their country. They did this instead of choosing what may have been best for themselves. A nation is blessed when God gives it leaders like these.

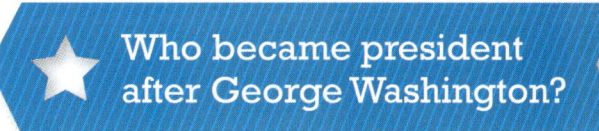

Who became president after George Washington?

4 Jefferson and Moving West

Focus
During Jefferson's presidency, the United States grew larger and became more democratic.

Election of 1800

In 1800, John Adams and Thomas Jefferson ran for president again. Some Federalists supported Adams. Most of the Democratic-Republicans wanted Jefferson to win. These two men and their political parties had different hopes for America's future.

Jefferson wanted more **democracy**, or rule by the people. He did not think that wisdom from the past was important for good government. He did not think that believing in God was important for good government. He thought giving people the freedom to choose what they wanted was good. Sometimes people make bad choices, but that is better than no choice at all.

The Cornell Farm, painting by Edward Hicks, 1848

Jefferson believed farmers were good people. They supported themselves on their own land. They did not need anyone to tell them what to do. Farmers had freedom. Jefferson did not support people in the trading business. Traders had to borrow money from banks. Traders depended on people to buy their goods. Jefferson did not think traders had freedom.

Jefferson also believed in freedom from religion. He did not want religion to be an important part of government. He said the government should not set aside special days for people to pray to God. Jefferson believed a man should be able to work in government whether he went to a church or not.

Adams and the Federalists disagreed with much of what Jefferson said. They liked democracy but were afraid of too much of it. They said that people sometimes make bad choices that hurt the entire country.

The Federalists liked farmers but said that traders were good too. America needed money to be strong. Trading made more money than farming. Federalists wanted the government to build roads, bridges, and canals. These would help traders and farmers. Federalists also wanted more banks. Banks could lend money to help new businesses.

Hand-colored copy of an Erie Canal print from the late 1800s

The Federalists favored religion in government. They wanted leaders to be moral. They thought religion helped people do what is right. Federalists said only people who believed the Bible should be part of a state government.

Adams and the Federalists thought that history taught good lessons. One lesson was that too much democracy can hurt a nation. This is because people are sinners. The Federalists thought Jefferson's ideas would not work.

Adams did what he believed was right. But there were Federalists who did not agree with him. They did not vote for him to be president again. **Thomas Jefferson** became the third president of the United States. This was the first time the country elected a president from a different political party.

In many countries, a change of political parties is not peaceful. But the change from Federalists to Democratic-Republicans in the election of 1800 was peaceful. This peaceful change set an important precedent for America.

What is one thing the Federalists wanted the government to do?

Natural Resources

Many people now lived in America. Jefferson and the Democratic-Republicans looked to the land in the West. They wanted the land in the West for farming. This land gave more space to build farms and towns.

Land is one of the most important natural resources. A **natural resource** is anything from nature that God created for people to use. Trees are another natural resource. Farmers used trees to build log cabins, barns, and fences.

Americans grew corn, tobacco, cotton, and other crops. They raised hogs, chickens, sheep, and cattle. At first, farmers raised crops just to feed their families. Later, farmers grew crops to sell in other places.

Water is also an important natural resource. Rivers provide water for crops and transportation. The Mississippi River was used to ship goods to the coast.

Natural Resources of the United States
Maine
Vermont
New Hampshire
Massachusetts
New York
Rhode Island
Connecticut
Wisconsin
Michigan
Pennsylvania
New Jersey
Ohio
Illinois
Indiana
West Virginia
Delaware
Virginia
Maryland
Kentucky
North Carolina
Tennessee
Mississippi River
South Carolina
ATLANTIC OCEAN
Mississippi
Alabama
Georgia
Florida
N
NW
NE
W
E
SW
SE
S
KEY
Cherries
Coal
Cotton
Maple syrup
Peanuts
Steel & iron
Chickens
Copper
Dairy cattle
Natural gas
Potatoes
Tobacco
Citrus fruits
Corn
Fish
Oil
Soybeans
Trees

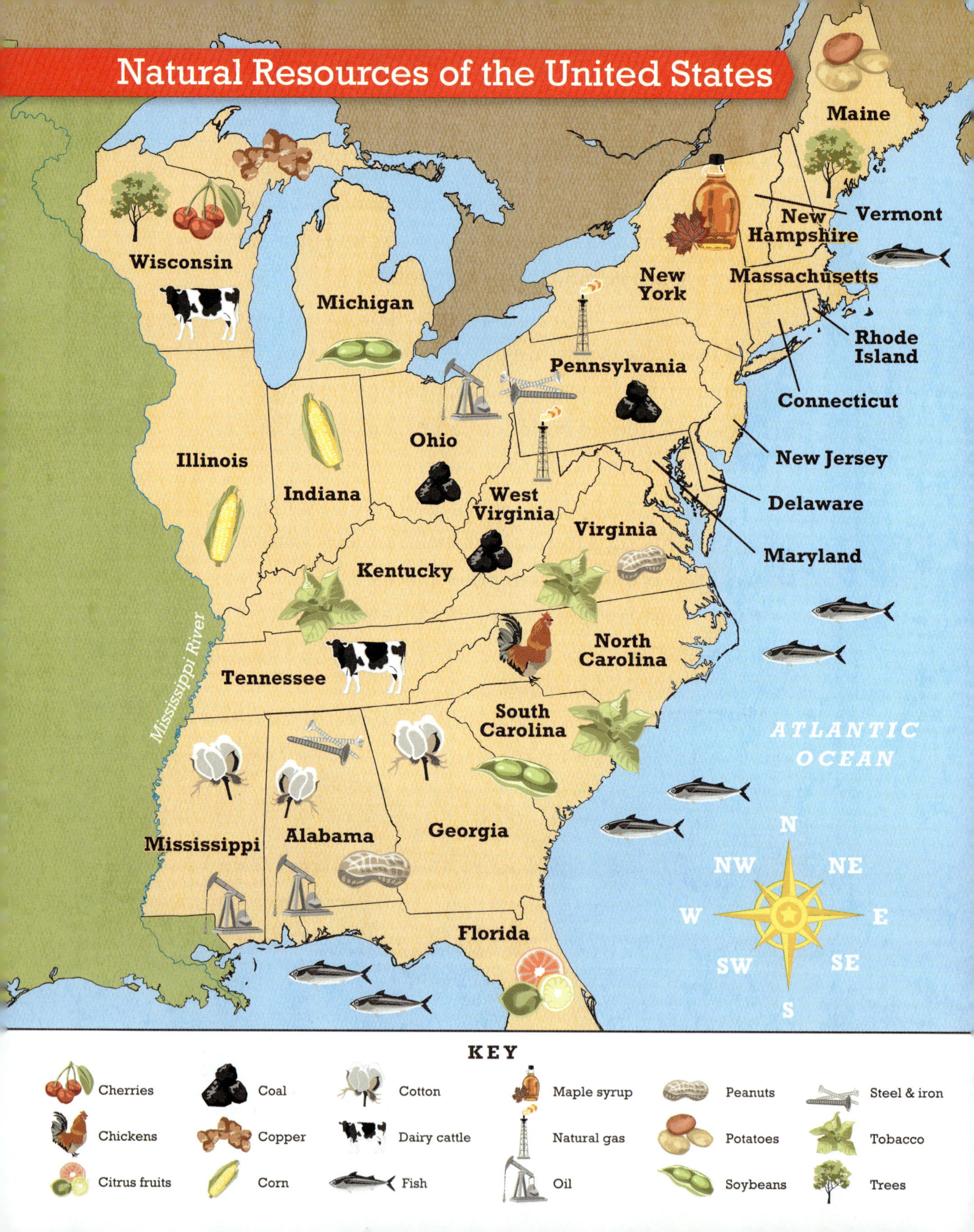

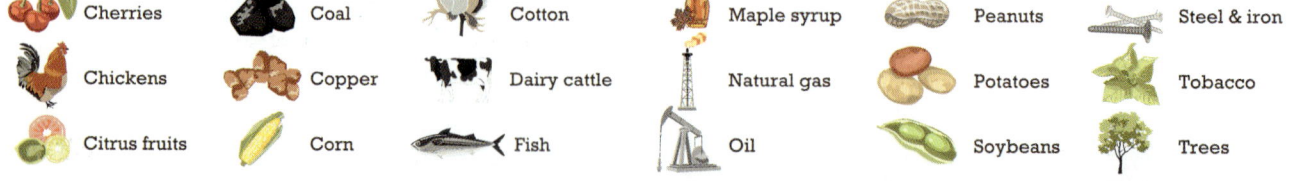

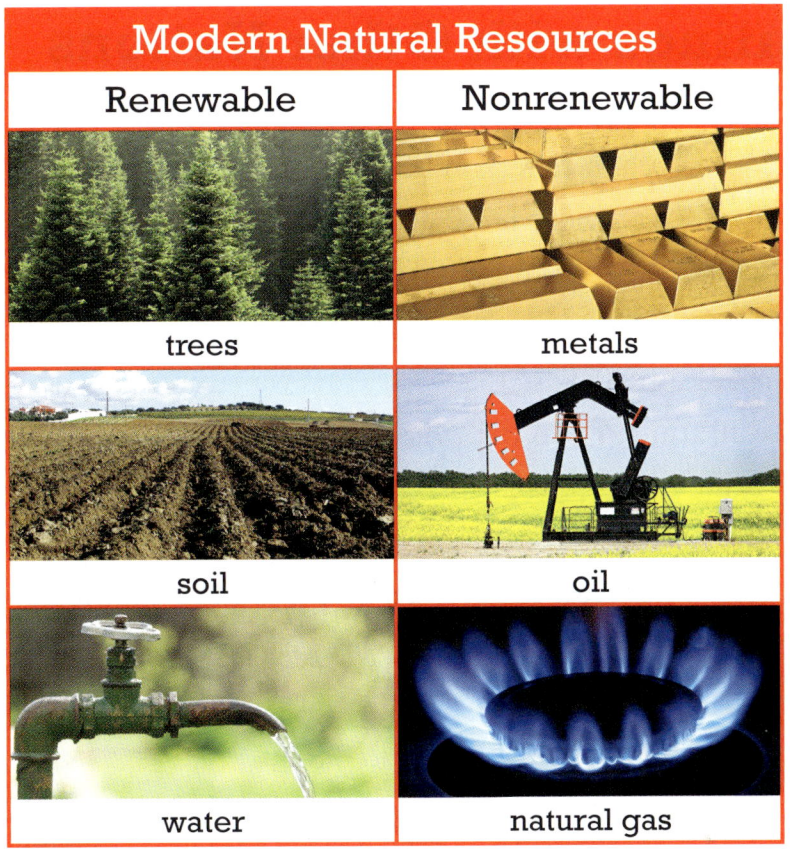

Modern Natural Resources	
Renewable	Nonrenewable
trees	metals
soil	oil
water	natural gas

Many resources are renewable resources. A **renewable resource** can be made again naturally. Crops such as corn or cotton are renewable resources. They can be harvested and then grown again the next year.

Some resources are nonrenewable. A **nonrenewable resource** is a natural resource that no longer forms today. Coal is a nonrenewable resource. There is only so much of it. When all the coal is mined from a certain place, it is gone.

★ What is a natural resource?

Dealings with Other Nations

The **Mississippi River** was the western border of the United States when Jefferson became president. Beyond the Mississippi River was a large area known as the **Louisiana Territory**. The most important city in this area was **New Orleans**. It was located at the end of the Mississippi River, near the Atlantic Ocean. New Orleans was important because all trade down the Mississippi River to the Atlantic Ocean came through this city.

The French had control of New Orleans. The French could keep American ships from going to the Atlantic Ocean. Jefferson wanted to buy New Orleans. Then the Americans would not need French permission to move goods through the city.

Louisiana Territory

Congress gave Jefferson the money to buy New Orleans. Jefferson sent men to France to talk about the purchase. France surprised Jefferson. It wanted to sell not only New Orleans but also all of the Louisiana Territory. France offered a good price for both.

Jefferson saw the benefits of buying both. The Americans would own New Orleans, and trade from the Mississippi River would not be cut off. The extra land in the territory would give space for farmers.

Jefferson sent the treaty for the final sale to Congress. Its members voted and approved the treaty. As a result of this sale in 1803, the United States more than doubled its size. This purchase was called the **Louisiana Purchase**.

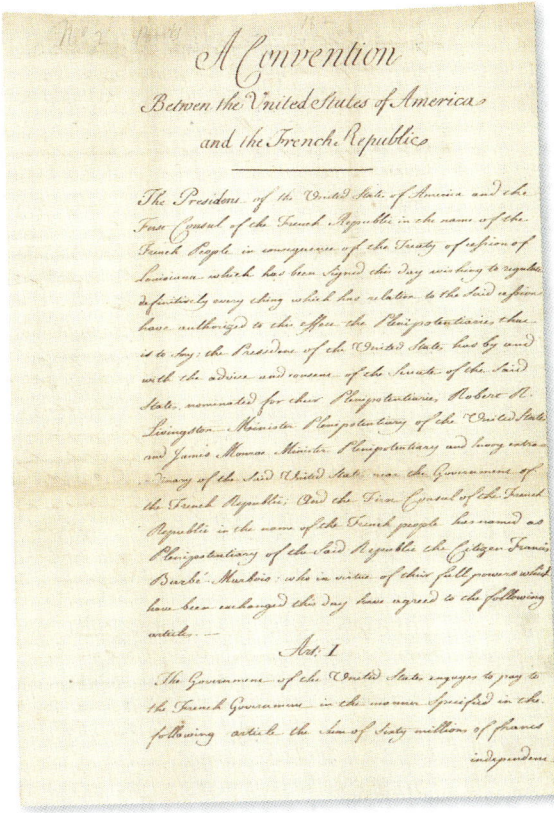

One of the documents for the Louisiana Purchase, 1803 (cover shown below)

Jefferson could not spend all of his time thinking about the West. He had some other concerns. Many other nations did not respect the United States because it was a young nation. The United States wanted to gain the respect of the world. The United States gained that respect in how it handled the war with the Barbary pirates.

The Barbary pirates attacked ships that brought goods across the ocean for trade. Some nations paid the pirates to not attack their ships. But this was expensive. Large nations, such as England and France, paid the pirates and were safe. But small nations could not afford to pay the pirates. So the pirates kept attacking ships from these small nations.

Jefferson did not want to pay the pirates. Neither did he want Americans to be captured and made slaves by the pirates. Jefferson needed a navy to fight the pirates. But he had kept the US military small. Jefferson believed that armies and navies led to wars. He also believed that armies

Bombardment of Tripoli, painted by Michele Felice Corne, 1804

USS Enterprise Capturing the Tripoli, drawn by Captain William Bainbridge Huff, around 1878

and navies put the people's freedom in danger. In some countries, armies took over their government. Jefferson was against having a standing army. This is the kind of army that the government keeps ready to fight even when there is not a war going on. But now America faced a war with pirates.

The small American navy began to fight the pirates. The American sailors were brave and skillful. One night they crept into a heavily armed harbor. They set a ship on fire. Even the powerful European nations recognized that Americans fought well. The pirates recognized it too. They signed treaties with the United States. They promised not to attack American ships anymore. The United States had earned the respect of the world.

What country did the United States buy the Louisiana Territory from?

Lewis and Clark

The Louisiana Purchase gave the United States a large amount of land. Jefferson sent men on an expedition to find out more about the Louisiana Territory. An **expedition** is a long trip to explore an unknown area. Jefferson picked **Meriwether Lewis** and **William Clark** to lead the expedition. Lewis knew about Indian ways and how to live in the woods. He knew about animals and plants. Clark was a soldier. He knew how to lead men, make maps, and measure the land.

Jefferson was interested in science and discovery. He told Lewis and Clark to take careful notes. He told them to draw the different plants and animals they saw. He also wanted them to have friendly meetings with the Indians. Lewis and Clark were to learn about the Indian ways of life.

Jefferson also had another reason for the Lewis and Clark expedition. He wanted to know what was past the Louisiana Territory. There was more land that went all the way to the Pacific Ocean. The United States might be able to claim that land.

Throughout the expedition, Lewis and Clark presented Jefferson Peace Medals to the Indians.

In the spring of 1804, Lewis and Clark left the city of Saint Louis. They traveled up the Missouri River. There were about forty men in their group. Clark's personal slave, York, went with them. York was the first black person that the Indians met. York was an important member of the expedition. He was skilled in hunting and scouting.

The group traveled through lands where trappers and traders had already been. Then the group moved into lands where Americans had not been before. People who spoke the Indian languages helped the men in the expedition talk to the Indians.

Lewis and Clark at Three Forks, painted by E. S. Paxson, 1912

Journal entries by Lewis and Clark, 1805 (left) and 1806 (right)

By winter the group reached what is now called North Dakota. Lewis and Clark sent some of the men home to report their discoveries. The others built a fort to live in during the winter.

In the spring, the group set out again. They were joined by an Indian named Sacagawea, her husband, and their baby. Sacagawea spoke an Indian language, and her husband could translate it to the group. The couple helped the group talk to other Indians along the way. Being able to talk to Indian tribes gave the group a chance to trade with them.

Soon the group crossed the Rocky Mountains. This was the hardest part of the journey. Then the group traveled down different rivers. They traveled all the way to the Pacific Ocean. These explorers were the first Americans to cross the entire North American continent. Afterward, they returned to Saint Louis. The expedition had taken two years and four months. Lewis and Clark kept journals of all the plants and animals they discovered. The journals showed that the men had discovered 178 new plants and 122 different animals.

Lewis & Clark Expedition, 1804–1806

What were the purposes of the Lewis and Clark expedition?

Activity

Planning supplies for a trip

What food do you take on a long trip? Lewis and Clark were gone for over two years. There were not many places to restock their supplies. They had to plan what food and supplies to take. During their journey, the men needed to know what plants and animals were safe to eat.

John Marshall

The Supreme Court is made up of judges. They are called *justices*. The top judge is called the **chief justice**. John Marshall became chief justice just before Jefferson became president. Marshall set several precedents while he led the Supreme Court.

Marshall and Jefferson did not agree on many things. Marshall was a Federalist. Jefferson was a Democratic-Republican. The Democratic-Republicans controlled the presidency and the Congress, but not the Supreme Court.

John Marshall

What: chief justice of the United States
When: 1755–1835
Where: Virginia and Washington, DC

John Marshall served America in many ways. He is most famous for being the fourth chief justice of the Supreme Court. For over thirty-four years, he guided the Supreme Court in deciding cases. Marshall helped establish the Supreme Court as an equal third branch in government.

The Democratic-Republicans did not like the Supreme Court. It was the branch of government that was the least controlled by the people. The people did not elect Supreme Court justices. The president chose them. Then those justices served for life. When John Adams was president, he chose John Marshall to be the chief justice.

One change Marshall made in the Supreme Court was about clothes. Some judges wore wigs and bright robes. They wanted to look like English judges. But Marshall wore a simple black robe. Other judges followed his precedent.

English judge

US Supreme Court justice

Justices used to help the political parties they liked. But Marshall stopped this. He believed the Supreme Court justices should think about the Constitution. He said they should not try to help or hurt certain parties.

Marshall's most important change made the Supreme Court powerful. He said that the Supreme Court can decide if a law agrees with the Constitution. This idea is called judicial review. **Judicial review** means the Supreme Court oversees all laws. The justices review, or check, a law. If it does not agree with the Constitution, the law is thrown out. When this happens, Congress cannot change the Supreme Court's decision. Judicial review makes the Supreme Court powerful.

United States Capitol, 1846

United States Supreme Court Building

Who was John Marshall?

Democracy

Government

The Federalists believed the people had a part to play in government. But the Federalists wanted a check on the people. Too much democracy was not good. People are sinners. The country could become immoral if the government did not put a check on the people.

The Democratic-Republicans thought differently. They thought too much government made people dishonest. Government workers would have more power and might become dishonest. The Democratic-Republicans thought these workers might be more honest if the government had less power.

Democracy began to grow stronger. It seemed to work. The Federalists' fears about democracy did not seem to come true. The Federalists never again won an election. By the 1820s the Federalist Party no longer existed.

The growth of democracy gave men a greater part in government. At first only white men who owned property could vote. Then white men without property were allowed to vote in the first half of the 1800s.

Election Day in Philadelphia, painted by John Lewis Kimmel, 1815

Church

Democracy had effects on churches. In the East, states stopped using taxes to support state churches. Democracy meant that people had freedom to choose. People chose which church to attend. They also wanted to choose which church to support.

After America became an independent nation, there was a revival. During that time many people came to know Christ. Some men who were newly saved wanted to become pastors. They often thought they did not need to go to school. They believed that any man who knew God and the gospel could preach without training. Many of these men traveled in the West. They started churches and held revival meetings. Their preaching helped the growth of Christianity in the United States.

Community

Another result of democracy was voluntary societies. A **voluntary society** is a group of people who try to solve problems. These people worked without pay. Some voluntary societies helped the poor or helped to improve prisons. Many voluntary societies were against slavery. Some made tracts, or papers that told of God's love. There were also voluntary societies who helped missionaries. These missionaries went around the world.

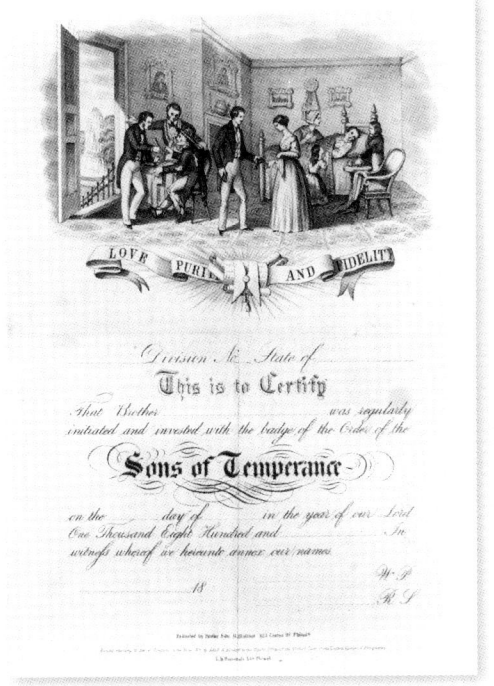

Certificate given to members of the Sons of Temperance, a voluntary society, 1857

Problems with Democracy

Sometimes people thought democracy meant they could ignore or disobey their authorities. Even in families or schools some people did not respect God's plan for leadership. At one college, students even burned buildings and tried to take control of the college.

Democracy had bad effects in churches. Some people thought they did not need to listen to their pastors. They could decide what to believe on their own. Many false religions began in the United States during the 1800s.

Effects of Democracy

	Government	Church	Community
Strengths	Places a check on elected officials	More preaching, causing Christianity to grow	Voluntary societies form, meeting important needs.
	More people take an interest in making sure the country has good government.	No more tax-supported state churches, meaning less government influence in churches	Average people may become more involved in improving their communities.
		Average church members may take more active roles in ministry.	
Weaknesses	May cause disrespect or rebellion against authority	Members may not pay attention to their pastor's authority. They may be more open to false teaching.	May cause disrespect or rebellion against authority
	Anyone can be a leader in government no matter how little training he has.	Causes some to think training for the ministry is not necessary	Voluntary societies may start to do the work that churches should do.
		Christianity treated as merely one of many religions	

What is a voluntary society?

Gardens and Slaves

Jefferson enjoyed farming. He separated his land into several farms. Other people managed these farms for him. Tobacco was the main crop. Jefferson had a vegetable garden and fruit trees. He grew many different kinds of vegetables and fruits. Some of these plants were new to the United States. He kept careful records of what grew well.

Jefferson's house was on a little mountain. He grew his garden on the southern slope of the mountain. The south side had more warm sunshine for the plants, even in the wintertime.

Jefferson's home was called Monticello. He grew fruits and vegetables like lettuce, radishes, tomatoes, and gooseberries.

Jefferson paid close attention to his gardens. Slaves who worked for him ran his farms. In the South, the owners of large plantations owned many slaves. Owners of small farms had one or two slaves or none at all.

Many people began to doubt that slavery was right. The Americans had already fought a war for their freedom. They believed they had a right to be free. They believed all men were created equal. Buying and selling people no longer seemed right.

Jefferson said that slavery was not good for people's way of life. He thought slaves should be free. He helped make sure that slavery was not allowed in the Northwest Territory. But Jefferson kept slaves because he did not know how to run a plantation without them.

Jefferson never freed his own slaves. He knew slavery was not going away anytime soon. He stopped trying to end slavery. He thought it was good enough if the slaves were treated well.

Early photo of Isaac Jefferson, slave of Thomas Jefferson, taken by John Plumbe Jr., 1845

Jefferson said this about slavery: "We have the wolf by the ears, and we can neither hold him, nor safely let him go." Jefferson knew that slavery, or the "wolf," was wrong. But he believed the country needed slaves. He knew that in the future America would have to deal with the "wolf."

What animal did Jefferson use to describe slavery?

5 The War of 1812 & National Growth

Focus

In the early 1800s, the United States began to take its place among the nations of the world.

James Madison

Americans liked Thomas Jefferson as president. He could have won another election to serve for a third term. But Jefferson thought Washington made the right choice to serve for only two terms. Jefferson did not run for a third term. Instead, he helped his friend James Madison become president.

James Madison did many important things before he became the fourth president. He had already shaped the nation. He had helped write the Constitution and the Bill of Rights, and he encouraged people to accept them. For years, he helped lead the Democratic-Republicans in Congress. Madison and Jefferson worked closely together.

Madison faced a big problem when he became president. Other countries did not always treat the United States fairly since it was a new country. At this time, Britain and France were fighting with each other. This had an effect on American trade. When the Americans traded with the French, the British got angry. When the Americans traded with the British, the French got angry. Both countries stopped American ships from trading. Sometimes Britain took American sailors.

Congress tried to solve the problem. Congress said that America would not trade with any country that stopped American trade ships. But when America stopped selling goods to countries, the national government made less money. The government could not pay its bills.

Painting of the *Leopard*, a British warship, firing on the *Chesapeake*, an American warship

War with Britain

James Madison was part of the Democratic-Republicans. They were angry at how Britain acted. Many thought Britain acted like America still belonged to Britain. The British stopped US trade ships and took US sailors. In Canada the British supplied weapons to the Indians to fight Americans. The Democratic-Republicans thought the United States should fight Britain. In 1812 the United States declared war on Britain.

Documents announcing the war with Great Britain

The War of 1812 had begun. Neither the United States nor Britain was ready to fight. The British were already fighting France. Britain did not want to fight two wars at the same time. The United States did not have a regular army. The Democratic-Republicans thought armies during peace were dangerous. Armies also cost a lot of money. The Democratic-Republicans only wanted to have an army once a war began.

Battle of Tippecanoe, lithograph by Kurz and Allison, about 1889

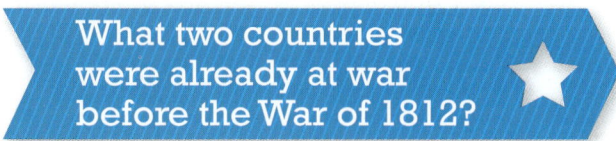

What two countries were already at war before the War of 1812?

Canada

When the war began, Americans knew where to start fighting. They wanted to defeat the British in Canada. It was a powerful colony of Britain. Britain often traded with Canada instead of the United States. More importantly, the British in Canada supplied weapons to the Indians in the United States.

The Americans thought taking over Canada would be easy. There were few British soldiers in Canada. Americans hoped that Canadians might join the United States. Americans thought Canadians wanted freedom from Britain.

Battle of Queenston Heights, the first major battle in the War of 1812

Fort Mackinac was the location of two battles for control of the Great Lakes during the War of 1812. Today the fort is a museum.

The Americans' hopes soon fell. Canadians did not join the American side. The American generals attacked Canada from the Michigan Territory, which was close to Canada's capital. When the British fought back, one American general gave up his entire army. The Americans did not gain Canada. They also lost the Michigan Territory to the British.

The Americans tried again. They attacked Canada twice from New York. Both times the New York military would not help the US military in Canada. Without extra help, the US military was not strong enough. The United States could not take over Canada.

United States Navy

The American navy was more successful than the American army. The American navy had fewer than a dozen ships. But they were built stronger than most ships. The British navy had hundreds of ships, but they were spread all over the world. Most were too far away to fight the Americans.

On August 19, 1812, an American ship called the USS *Constitution* fought the British ship called the HMS *Guerriere*. The *Constitution* had heavier guns and did more damage to the *Guerriere*. Many British cannonballs bounced off the *Constitution*. People later called the ship "Old Ironsides." The British gave up. For the first time in this war, an American ship defeated a British ship.

America won several more sea battles. But the British still had the more powerful navy. They controlled the seas.

The USS *Constitution* defeating the HMS *Guerriere*

Fighting in the North

Americans were happy that the USS *Constitution* had defeated a British ship. But they were upset about losing the Michigan Territory. The British seemed to be winning the war. Before making a peace treaty with Britain, America wanted to get its lost land back.

The US Navy led the way. The navy wanted to win control of the Great Lakes. These lakes were part of the Michigan Territory. Without these lakes, Britain could not keep the Michigan Territory.

Oliver Hazard Perry commanded US Navy ships. He built a fleet of nine ships. It fought the British fleet on Lake Erie. The Americans won the battle even though Perry's own ship was destroyed.

After losing the battle, the British went back to Canada. American soldiers followed. There they defeated the British and the Indians who were helping them. An Indian leader called Chief Tecumseh died in battle.

Before the war, Chief Tecumseh had brought Indian tribes together to fight against the Americans. The Indians wanted the Americans to stop moving into Indian lands. After Chief Tecumseh's death, no other leader could unite the Indian tribes to fight the Americans.

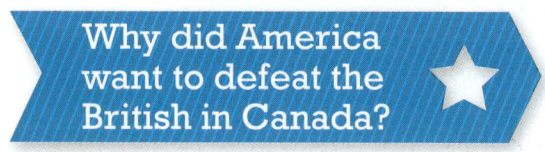

Why did America want to defeat the British in Canada?

British Attack the East

Just when America seemed to be winning, the British started to fight harder. By 1814 Britain had defeated France. Britain could now focus on the United States. The British attacked the eastern coast first. They wanted to take Washington, DC, because it was the US capital. They also wanted to control Baltimore, Maryland. Baltimore was an important port city.

The British did well in Washington, DC. Only a small force of Americans defended the city. They retreated when the British came. The British burned many buildings. They even burned the White House. The British said they wanted revenge on the Americans.

In Baltimore the British had less success. **Fort McHenry** guarded the harbor of Baltimore. British ships fired on the fort for twenty-five hours. Although cannons bombarded it continuously, the fort stood firm. The British finally left Baltimore when they saw that the Americans would not give up.

Aerial view of Fort McHenry

End of the War

Like the Americans, the British did not give up. They attacked northern New York from Canada. British ships sailed down a lake, and British soldiers marched by land. The Americans prepared well for the attack. They won the battle both on land and on water. The British realized they would not defeat the Americans. The American victory at this battle helped them in the peace talks with Britain.

In 1814 both sides agreed on a peace treaty. The war had come to a draw. But it took several weeks for this news to come to America. During this time, British troops attacked the American army at New Orleans. General Andrew Jackson commanded this army. Jackson's army was in a strong position, and the British could not win. Some pirates also helped Jackson. The American cannons destroyed the British army as it attacked, and the Americans won the Battle of New Orleans. By this time the peace treaty had already been signed. Both sides had already agreed to a draw. But winning the last battle was a successful end for the Americans.

Battle of New Orleans, painting by Jean Hyacinthe de Laclotte, who was there at the battle in 1815

Signing of the peace treaty between America and Britain, by Amédée Forestier, 1914

The peace treaty put everything back to the way it was before the war. No one gained any land. No one lost any land. All captured ships were returned. However, European countries began to respect America as a truly independent nation. America proved it could defend itself.

The war did change how America dealt with the Indians. The Americans had defeated the Indian nations. These nations lost land and fighting strength. The Americans did not always treat the Indians well. Andrew Jackson had defeated a group of Creek Indians and made them sign a treaty. The treaty took land away from all Creeks, even those who fought for the United States. This was against the law. President Madison ordered Jackson to return the land, but Jackson refused. Jackson was a popular war hero, so the United States government let him do what he wanted.

Why did the British want to control Washington, DC?

Patriotism

During the War of 1812, many Americans showed courage and love for their country. Love and faithfulness to one's country is called **patriotism**.

Dolley Madison was the president's wife. When the British attacked Washington, DC, she saved items from the White House. These included important papers and a painting of George Washington. Today that painting hangs in the White House.

Francis Scott Key, a lawyer, saw the large American flag flying over Fort McHenry when the British attacked the fort. He knew that as long as the flag flew, the Americans were unbeaten. He wrote the poem **"The Star-Spangled Banner."** It later became America's national anthem.

After the war, Americans were proud of their country. They had defended themselves against the most powerful nation. Americans remembered heroes who showed patriotism.

Folding the Flag

Did you know there is a special way the American flag is folded? It is folded into the shape of a tri-cornered hat with thirteen folds. Each fold represents a religious principle upon which America was founded. The stars should be on the top fold. The flag should never touch the ground.

Future of the Nation

Madison's Plan

After the War of 1812, James Madison gave Congress a plan for the nation's future. Madison wanted the nation to learn from the war. He thought Congress needed to do three things.

First, Madison wanted a new Bank of the United States. Only Congress could set up a national bank. Madison believed the nation needed one. He found it hard to get money for the nation during the war. He thought the nation should be able to borrow money if the nation needed it.

Second, Madison asked Congress for a tariff. Setting a tariff, or a tax on imports, would help the new American factories. People would buy more American goods rather than imports.

Third, Madison wanted better **transportation**, or a way to move people or goods. During the war the military had trouble moving supplies because of bad roads. Now that the war was over, America needed good roads for trade.

Boston Manufacturing Company, a mill on the Charles River, Waltham, Massachusetts

The Erie Canal runs from the Hudson River in Albany, New York, to Lake Erie in Buffalo, New York. The canal connects the Atlantic Ocean to the Great Lakes.

Madison did not think the law allowed the national government to pay for roads and canals. So he wanted Congress to pass an **amendment**, or a change to the Constitution. He wanted the Constitution to allow the national government to give money for improving transportation.

Need for Tariffs

Before the war, few Americans were manufacturers. A **manufacturer** is someone who makes goods, such as cloth. Americans often bought things made in Britain. But the war made it hard for Americans to get British imports. So Americans began to make their own goods.

After the war, the British wanted America to buy their goods again. The British made less money when Americans made and sold their own goods. So British manufacturers planned to sell their goods in America at low prices. But if people bought fewer American goods, American factories would lose money and have to close. Madison knew a tariff would help keep American factories open. He believed this and the other ideas he gave Congress would help America.

Congress Acts

Some people did not agree with Madison's ideas and tried to stop them. But many liked his ideas. Henry Clay and John C. Calhoun helped the most. They led others in Congress to back Madison's plan. Clay called it the **American System**. The plan included a national bank, a tariff, and improvements in transportation.

Calhoun and Clay worked together in Congress to set up the Second Bank of the United States. The bank would help both government and businesses. The bank could lend money to the government during times of war or other problems. The bank could also lend money to businesses to create new jobs. Roads, canals, or factories could be built using money from the bank.

Calhoun backed Madison's idea of having a tariff. It would help protect American manufacturers from unfair British trade. Congress agreed to having a tariff.

The Second Bank of the United States, located in Philadelphia, Pennsylvania

But not everyone in Congress agreed that the Constitution should be changed to allow for Madison's plan. Congress did not pass an amendment to improve transportation. Instead, Congress simply sent Madison a bill. A **bill** is a statement of rules that Congress wants to become a law. This bill gave money to build roads and canals. Madison thought the Constitution did not let Congress spend money for transportation. So he vetoed the bill. To **veto** means to refuse a bill.

These events happened while Madison served for two terms as the fourth president.

What were Madison's plans for the nation's future?

A discussion between President Monroe and his cabinet, painting by Allyn Cox, 1973–1974

Monroe Doctrine

After Madison served two terms, Americans elected **James Monroe** as the fifth president of the United States. He worked to help other countries.

Monroe wanted European nations to leave the new countries in the Americas alone. Many of these countries gained their independence from Spain in the early 1800s. The United States wanted these new countries to stay independent.

Monroe worked with John Quincy Adams, the secretary of state. They made a plan to protect the independent nations in the Americas. The plan was called the **Monroe Doctrine**. It said that European nations should not form new colonies in the Americas. Also, European nations should not bother independent countries there. The United States promised it would not bother European nations.

Monroe's presidency was peaceful. The Democratic-Republicans controlled the government. They were the only party. Some thought the days of fighting between parties were over. But as the country grew, problems started.

More settlers moved southwest after the War of 1812. They settled on the land taken from the Creek and the Cherokee Indians. The land was rich and good for crops. Southern farmers and plantation owners grew enough food to support themselves and to send exports to other countries. Out of all the crops, cotton made the most money. Some food crops went bad before farmers could sell them. Cotton could be stored without going bad. It grew in many kinds of soil. But cotton took a lot of work to plant, pick, and clean. Slaves did this work.

Differences in the North and South

Early American leaders hoped that slavery would slowly go away. Then life changed. The South grew more cotton, and many people thought slavery was necessary. Southerners stopped wanting slavery to end.

At the same time, the North grew fewer crops. It focused on shipping and manufacturing. Northerners built factories, roads, and canals.

Differences	
North	South
shipping and manufacturing	grew crops
factories, roads, canals	plantations and farms
wanted high tariffs	wanted low tariffs

Northerners and southerners had different ways of life. Each wanted the national government to act differently. Northerners wanted high tariffs. They wanted to protect their factories from European trade. Southerners wanted low tariffs. They wanted to sell their cotton to Europe. If the United States placed high tariffs on other countries' goods, those countries might do the same to southern cotton. If the cotton became expensive for other countries, fewer people might buy it. Then the South would make less money.

Missouri Compromise

In 1819, Missouri wanted to join the nation as a slave state. Missouri was a settled part of the territory that used to be called the Louisiana Territory. At this time there were eleven free states and eleven slave states. If one more state were added, there would not be a balanced number anymore. Also, there would be more slave states than free states.

Northern states did not want Missouri to be a slave state. They thought this would give slave states too many votes in Congress. Slave states in the South wanted low tariffs. If the slave states had control in Congress, tariffs might be lowered. This would harm manufacturing in the North.

The South did not want Missouri to be a free state. If it were, free states would likely form in the territory near Missouri. There would be more free states than slave states in the United States. Southerners feared that northerners would control Congress and tell southerners how to live.

Before the Compromise

After the Compromise

Finally, Congress came up with a compromise. Two new states would join. Missouri entered as a slave state. Maine joined as a free state. Maine used to be part of Massachusetts. Now Congress would have a balance. Congress would have representatives from twelve free states and twelve slave states.

Congress added another rule to the compromise. A line was drawn west of Missouri's southern border. Any future state north of the line would be free. States south of the line could be slave or free. Congress hoped that the **Missouri Compromise** would be a permanent solution to the slave problem. But America still faced challenges. The northerners and the southerners trusted each other less.

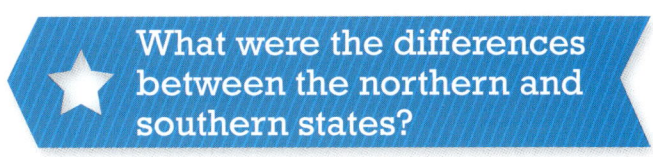

What were the differences between the northern and southern states?

American Communities

Americans continued to move westward. They moved from the East to settle in the West. They settled in different places and developed communities. A community is a place where people live and work together. Americans lived in two kinds of communities: urban and rural.

An **urban community** is usually called a city. New York, Philadelphia, and New Orleans were the largest American urban communities at that time. Cities have many people, jobs, buildings, and kinds of transportation.

A **rural community** is outside the city. Houses are farther apart. At that time many people in rural areas were farmers. The towns in rural communities are smaller than cities. Today most rural communities have schools, churches, and stores.

Communication

Communities in America grew. As Americans spread across the continent, they wanted to be connected. People moved far from their families. They needed more post offices to send and receive letters. The mail also brought newspapers. People in different places could read about what was going on in the world. Both urban and rural communities had a postal service.

Transportation

People from rural communities sold crops to people in urban communities. To move these crops, people needed good transportation. But building and taking care of roads cost a lot of money. Wagons carried goods but were slow and expensive. Transporting, or moving, goods by water was cheaper and faster. But few rural communities in the Northwest were located by a river that flowed to a big city.

Government leaders in New York thought of a way to make water transportation easier. They built the Erie Canal to connect the Great Lakes and the Atlantic Ocean. A **canal** is a manmade waterway that connects two bodies of water. Most canals are shallow. They are at least four feet deep. Transporting goods from the east became cheaper.

Ohio, Indiana, and Pennsylvania also built canals. Soon canals connected much of the Northwest to the Northeast. People and trade easily moved back and forth.

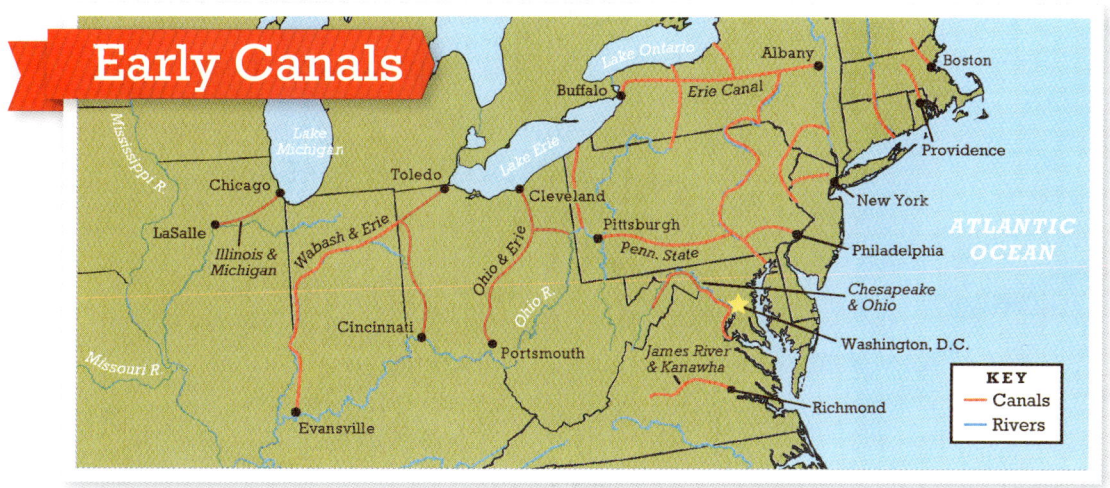

Early Canals

Inventions

Canals were not the only change in transportation. The invention of the steam engine made moving people and goods easier. This type of engine was powered by steam. The steam engine was used in machines like boats and trains.

The Clermont, a steamboat built by Robert Fulton (engineer and inventor)

The steamboat changed how people and goods traveled. Before the steamboat, boats mostly carried goods down a river, in the direction it flowed. Carrying goods against the river current was harder. However, steamboats were more powerful because they had a steam engine. Steamboats easily moved against a river current. Now people and goods went up and down rivers. Steamboats became an important part of America's transportation. They helped western settlement and trade.

Tom Thumb, the first American-built steam locomotive, designed and built by Peter Cooper in 1830

Trains powered by the steam engine made railroads possible. Railroads added a faster and cheaper way of transportation. They were also reliable. Snow, flood, and drought had little effect on trains. In time, the railroad became the main means of transportation in America.

Canals, steamboats, and trains helped Americans receive news and goods from far-off places. These inventions let people move around the country more easily. If a family had a hard time making a living in one area, they could move to a new place. New inventions and improvements helped Americans be independent and free.

What advantage did the steamboat have over ordinary boats?

Business in the Northeast

Northeastern states are sometimes called the New England states. Most people who settled in these states were from Britain. Before the War of 1812, shipping, or transporting trade goods by ship, was the most important business in the Northeast. Whaling was another important business there. People used whale blubber to make oil and candles. People also used whalebone to make objects, such as glasses and tools.

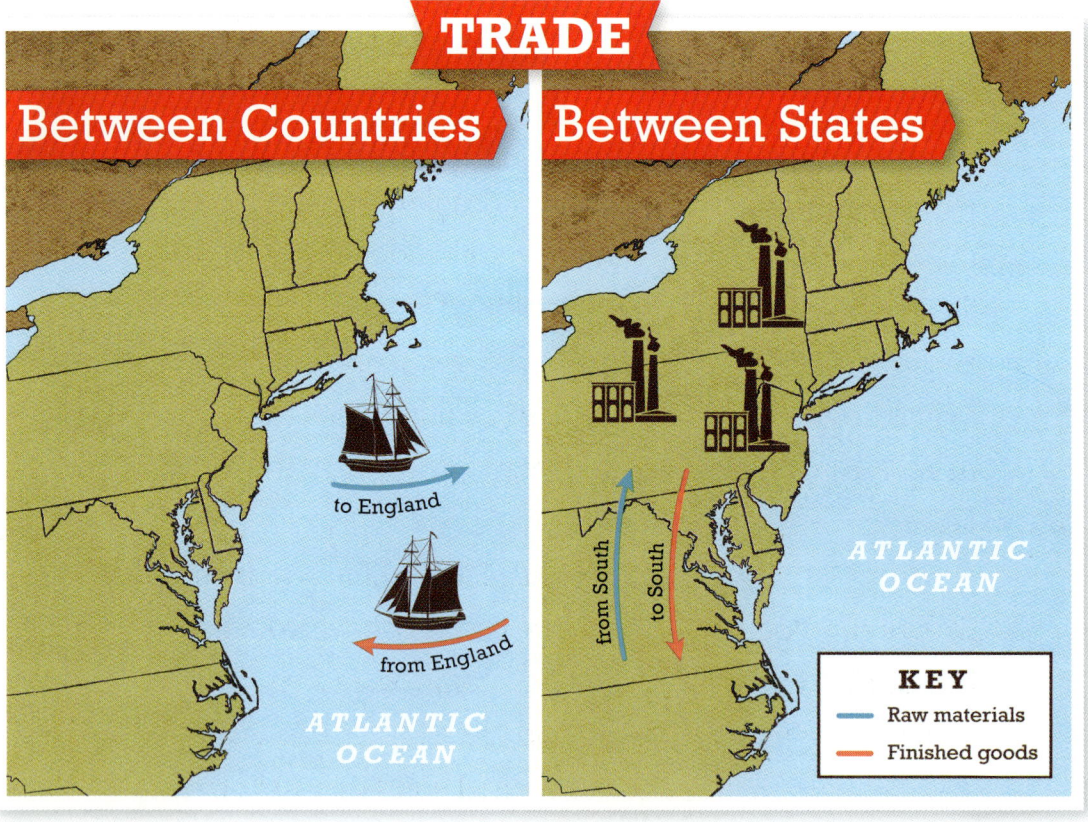

Slater Mill on the Blackstone River in Pawtucket, Rhode Island

Many more factories opened in the Northeast. There were several reasons. First, New England states had fast-moving streams. These could provide power for factories. Second, many people were looking for work. The New England states had a short growing season for farming. Winters were long, and there were fewer jobs then. Many people, especially young women, found work in the factories.

People in New England built factories to produce goods. Before the War of 1812, goods were shipped from England. But during the war fewer goods came from there. Factories in New England began to produce more goods. After the war, New England factories turned southern cotton into yarn or cloth.

At first a factory made only one kind of product. For example, a factory might simply make yarn. Workers were hired to knit the yarn into cloth or clothing in their homes.

Soon factories took over the whole process of making goods. Workers no longer worked in their homes but in factories. People needed to live closer to the factories. Some factory owners built villages for their workers.

Mill town, 1861 (present-day Stoddard, New Hampshire)

Work in the factories was hard. Work hours were long. Factories were sometimes dangerous and unhealthy. Many children worked in the factories. They worked Monday through Saturday. They had no time to go to school.

Christian leaders and parents wanted children to learn how to read and write. Some people started Sunday schools to teach children. In Sunday schools, children learned to read and write. They also learned about God and the Bible. Samuel Slater started one of the first Sunday schools in the United States. He owned a factory, and he wanted his workers to learn about God.

God's Blessings

The War of 1812 made the United States sure of its independence from Great Britain. But some American citizens did not act rightly. Some treated the American Indians and black Americans badly. This would cause problems in the future. But God blessed Americans with many natural resources and skills. He also blessed America with a growing number of Christians who wanted to please God.

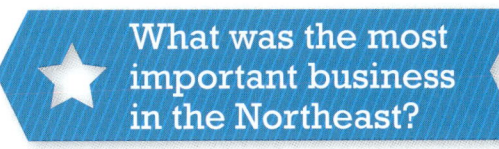
What was the most important business in the Northeast?

6 Andrew Jackson & Democracy

Focus

Many changes in American democracy happened during Andrew Jackson's presidency.

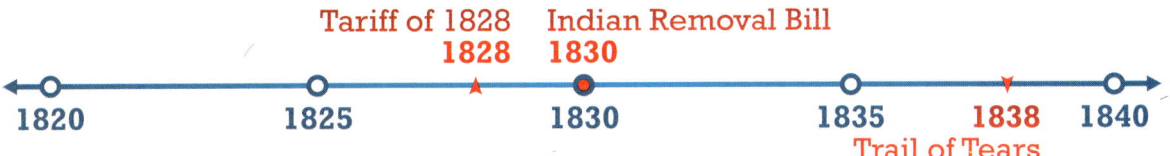

Election of 1824

In 1824 four men ran for president. But this election was different from earlier elections. None of the men won enough votes in the Electoral College. When this happens, the House of Representatives has to decide who will be president.

Two of the men seemed most likely to win. Andrew Jackson had the most votes from the people. Most Americans remembered Jackson's victory over the British in the War of 1812. John Quincy Adams won the second-most votes. He had served the government for a long time.

Henry Clay was one of the four men who ran for president. He got only a few votes. But he was in a good position. He led the House of Representatives. Clay could help select the winner. He did not trust Jackson. He remembered that Jackson did not always obey the law. Clay wanted the best president possible. He thought Adams had served the nation well. **John Quincy Adams** became the sixth president of the United States.

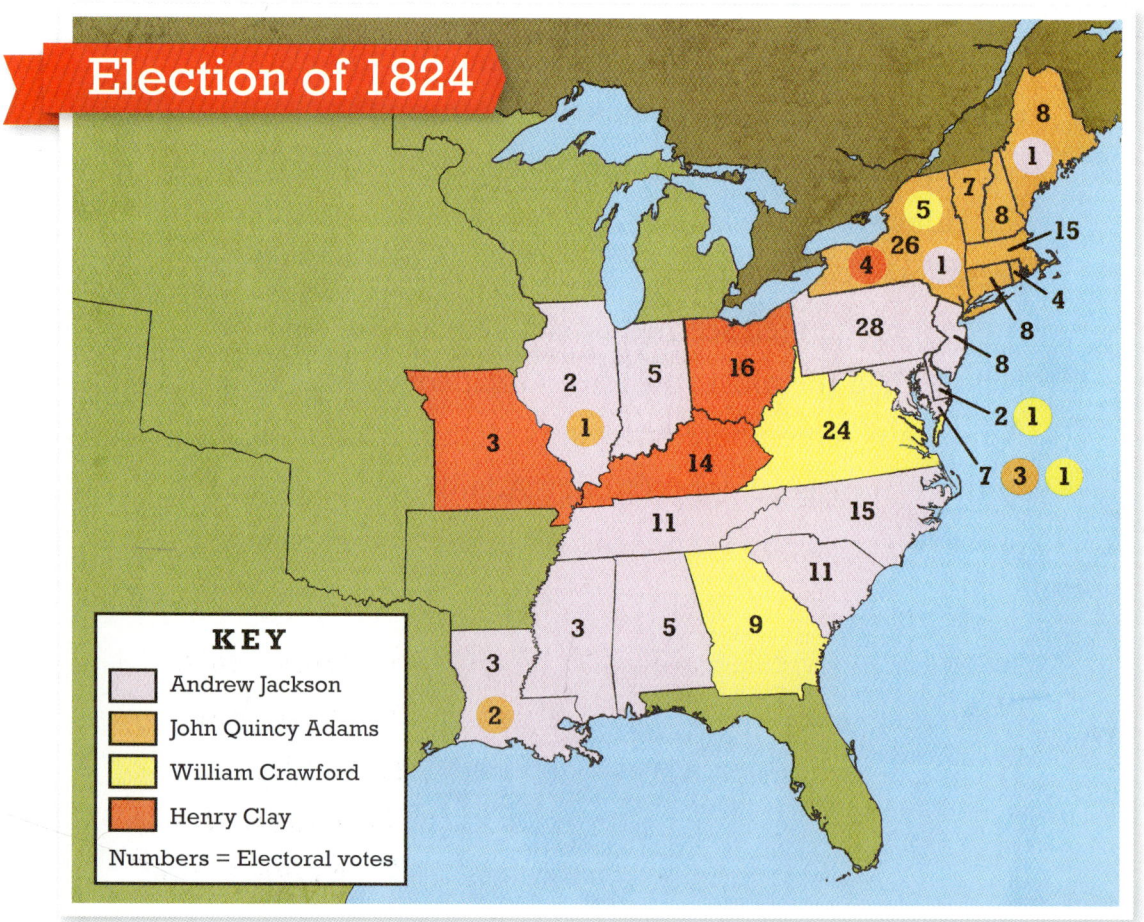

Presidential Candidates of 1824

Andrew Jackson

John Quincy Adams

William Crawford

Henry Clay

John Quincy Adams chose Henry Clay to be the secretary of state. Jackson said the two men planned this. He said the men had made a corrupt, or dishonest, deal. Jackson said the men helped each other get their jobs. Adams said this was not true. He said he chose the best man for the job. But for the next four years, Jackson complained about Adams and Clay.

Adams and His Plans

Adams made big plans. He wanted to sell land in the west. He wanted to use that money to build roads and canals. He wanted a stronger army and navy. He wanted the United States to use a measuring system called the metric system. He wanted to build a college in Washington, DC. Adams tried to make every part of the country better.

Jackson's followers did not like Adams's plans. They would cost too much. Money for the plans would come from taxes. Some did not think all Americans should pay taxes for plans that helped only some people. Some thought the Constitution did not even allow the plans. In the end, Congress did not act on Adams's plans.

If the Electoral College cannot decide who wins an election, who does decide?

Election of 1828

Adams and Jackson ran against each other in the 1828 election. Jackson said he wanted to have honest leaders. He said leaders in government were not being honest. He wanted the people to have more say in their government.

Jackson spread his message through newspapers. They told of his plans and what he thought about Adams. The news spread across the country. Newspapers became a new way to spread news about men running for president.

Jackson's followers told others to vote for him. Jackson won the most votes. He also won enough votes in the Electoral College. Andrew Jackson won the election and became the next president of the United States.

Jackson said he would put honest government workers in office. He wanted men who agreed with his plans. Many wanted to work in Jackson's government.

On the day Jackson took office, many people came to the White House. Many of them wanted government jobs. Some thought the crowds showed that Jackson was the people's president. People believed he cared about them. Others were worried that Jackson would choose people to work for him who could not do the job.

Jackson's first inauguration

Jackson's second inauguration

Democracy and Government Jobs

Andrew Jackson and John Quincy Adams did not agree on who should serve in government. Adams thought that it should be the person with the best skills. It did not matter if the person supported, or favored, a different man for president. That person was still the best one to do the job.

Jackson thought differently. He thought government jobs did not need special skills. He thought the best people for government jobs were his followers. They had the same ideas that he had about governing the country.

Hiring Government Workers	
John Quincy Adams	Hire people with the best skills
Andrew Jackson	Hire people who support the president

Jackson also said that people should work government jobs only for a few years. Then new people could take those jobs. He believed that changing workers helped stop dishonesty in government jobs.

Jackson found out that some government workers were dishonest. Some had stolen thousands of dollars from the treasury. These workers were sent to prison. But Jackson also removed government workers who had done nothing wrong. He gave their jobs to his followers. He said that anyone could do these jobs. Jackson thought this brought more democracy to government. Some people did not agree with Jackson's changes. These people did not think he should give jobs only to those who supported him. Good workers could lose their jobs.

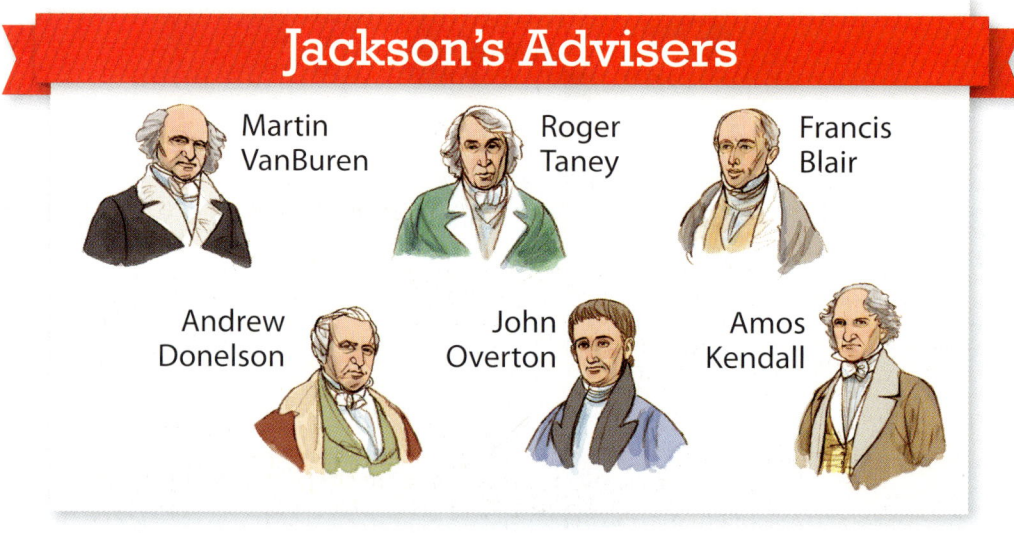

Jackson's Advisers

Martin VanBuren

Roger Taney

Francis Blair

Andrew Donelson

John Overton

Amos Kendall

How were Jackson and Adams different in hiring government workers?

Democracy and Religion

Since the time of the Revolutionary War, Christians favored democracy. They favored democracy in government and also in religion.

People believed they should read the Bible and decide for themselves what it taught. This belief had both good and bad results.

Democracy in religion helped education. People had more freedom to read and learn the Bible. Christians and churches started schools throughout the country. Missionaries started schools for American Indians and for free black Americans.

Many states did not allow slaves to attend school. Some masters did not teach their slaves to read or write. These masters thought that slaves who could read were more likely to rebel. But some masters taught their slaves to read. These masters believed that everyone should be able to read the Bible.

Sioux boys at the Carlisle Indian School, Pennsylvania, 1879

Sometimes democracy in religion was not good. Many thought about the Bible in a way that pleased them. Many also lost respect for their pastors. It did not matter that their pastors had been trained to study the Bible. Some people did not trust their pastors' teachings and thought pastors were not needed. These ways of thinking led to several false religions. In the Northeast, some pastors stopped believing God's Word. They preached that Jesus was not God. They did not accept the Bible's authority.

Some Christian leaders saw that democracy in religion could be good and bad. These leaders wanted to keep the good things about democracy. Freedom of religion allowed people to practice their beliefs. Christians were free to read and study the Bible. They started schools. Many Christians joined voluntary societies and helped people. But people also had freedom to follow false teachers of religion. Christian leaders saw the need for pastors to be trained to teach God's truth.

The Shakers were one community who followed beliefs not found in the Bible.

Hand-colored woodcut of Princeton Seminary, New Jersey, 1850s

Some pastors started Princeton Seminary. A **seminary** is a school to train pastors. They learn from older Christians. For many years, Princeton Seminary helped pastors to learn and know God's truth.

Godly leaders also taught creeds. A **creed** is a statement of what a church believes the Bible teaches. One creed says, "There is but one only, living, and true God, Who is infinite in being and perfection." Creeds help Christians to recognize false teaching. Some churches make their pastors and members agree to a creed. A Bible-based creed helps keep false teachers out of the church.

Democracy in American Christianity had good results. Many studied the Bible and lived a Christian life. Democracy in religion also had bad results. Some people did not think rightly about the Bible. Some people stopped listening to pastors who taught the truth. Some did not respect the wisdom of Christians from the past. Many false religions started. But even during all this, many people read God's Word more. God was working in America.

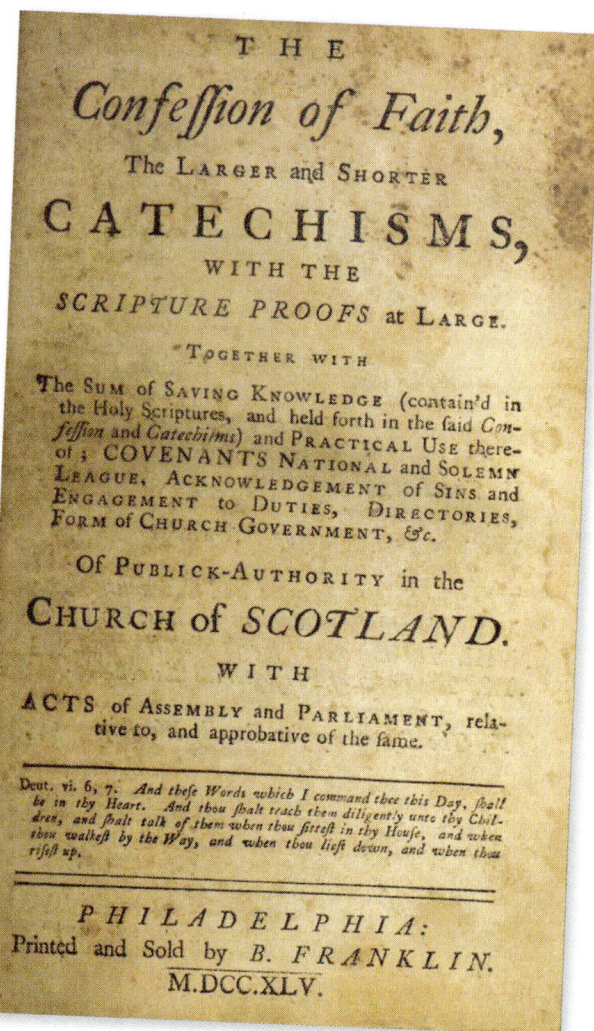

Cover page for the Westminster Confession of Faith, an early church creed

What is a seminary?

144

Spread of Christianity

Christianity grew in the early 1800s. Christians spread the gospel. Missionaries told the Indians about Christ.

Some Americans wanted to take the gospel to foreign countries. *Foreign* means outside one's own country. Adoniram Judson was the first missionary from the United States to serve in a foreign country. He was a

Adoniram Judson

foreign missionary to the country of Burma. He served there for thirty-seven years. He learned the Burmese language. He translated the Bible into Burmese. This Bible is used in Burma to this day.

Missionaries from the United States also went to Hawaii. They saw people trust in Christ. Often, new believers told others of Christ. One of the new believers was Kapiolani. She was part of the royal family. She had a church built for her people to learn more about God.

Kapiolani

What: Hawaiian chiefess
When: about 1781–1841
Where: Hawaii

High Chiefess Kapiolani was a member of the Hawaiian nobility. She eagerly accepted missionaries. She attended their school, where she learned to read and write. She had a boat bring a preacher for services at the church she had built. Kapiolani showed her new faith by turning against false gods.

Kapiolani showed the Hawaiians that their gods did not exist. The islands had active volcanoes. The people believed in a goddess of fire named Pele. People gave offerings to Pele so she would not be angry. People believed that volcanos erupted whenever Pele was angry. Kapiolani climbed a volcano. She went down into part of the volcano. But she did not give offerings to Pele. Instead, she prayed and confessed that God was the true God.

Who was the first American missionary to serve in a foreign country?

Understanding Hemispheres

The **equator** is drawn around the middle of the globe. The equator divides Earth into two parts. Each part is called a hemisphere. *Hemi* means "half." The half of Earth that is north of the equator is called the **Northern Hemisphere**. The half of Earth that is south of the equator is called the **Southern Hemisphere**. The **prime meridian** runs north and south on the globe. It divides the **Western Hemisphere** from the **Eastern Hemisphere**.

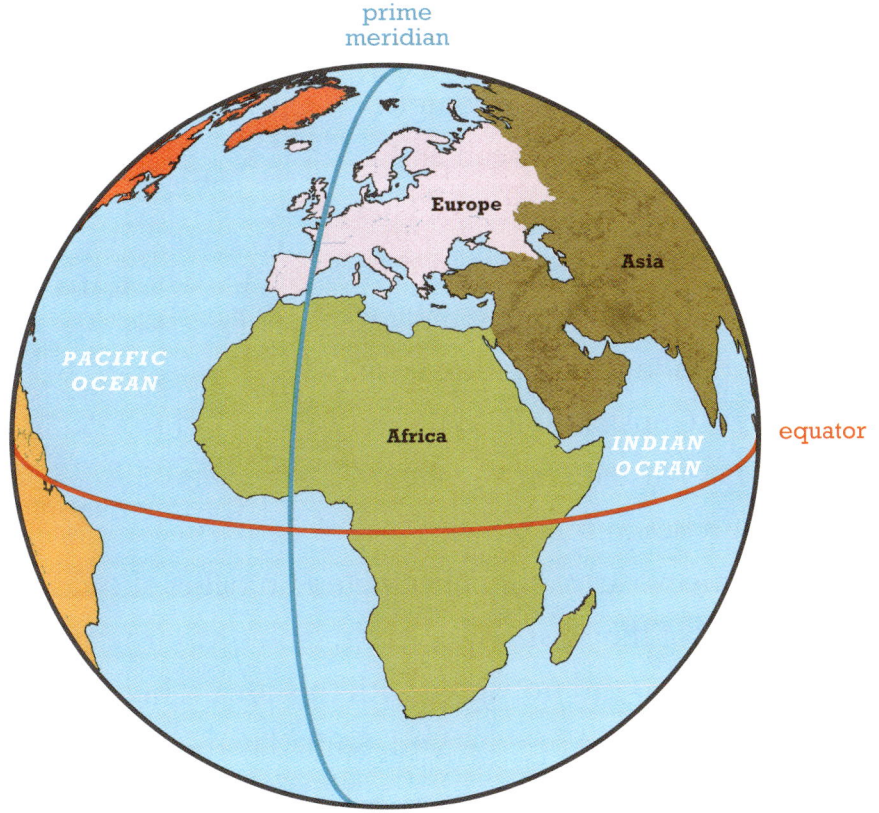

Broken Treaties

Many lands still belonged to Indian tribes when Andrew Jackson became president. The Cherokees were one of these tribes. After the Revolutionary War, the Cherokees made a peace treaty with the United States. After signing the treaty, the Cherokees never again fought against the United States. They helped the United States in the War of 1812.

The Cherokees built towns, farms, and mills on their land. They traded with settlers. A Cherokee named Sequoyah did an amazing thing. He developed the written Cherokee language. Cherokees could now read and write in their own language. They even printed a newspaper in their language. In 1827, they wrote a constitution for their nation based on the US Constitution. Many Cherokees trusted Christ. They built churches in their towns.

The Cherokee alphabet

Many Americans thought the Indian tribes should move west of the Mississippi River. James Monroe and John Quincy Adams did not agree with this idea. They thought the Indians should be educated. Someday the Indians could become United States citizens. But Andrew Jackson wanted the Indians to move west of the Mississippi River.

The Cherokees thought that they would be left alone by the United States. They had made treaties with the United States. These treaties promised that the Cherokees did not need to follow state laws. The Cherokees could pass their own laws. But after Jackson became president, life for the Indians changed. The state of Georgia told the Cherokees who lived there that they had to follow state law.

Indian Removal Bill

A new bill was written. It was called the Indian Removal Bill. It gave the president permission to give lands west of the Mississippi River to the Indians. The bill allowed the national government to pay for the move. Jackson signed it.

The bill did not force the Indians to move. But it said that the US government would stop protecting the Indians from people who might take their land. The only way for the Indians to keep their way of life was to move west. Many tribes decided to move west, but the Cherokees did not.

Many Christians thought the removal plan was wrong. Some Christians wrote newspaper articles and tracts about Indian rights. Missionaries to the Cherokees defended the Indians' right to stay.

Georgia told all missionaries to leave Cherokee lands that Georgia claimed. Missionaries who did not leave were put in jail. Their case was taken to the Supreme Court.

The court said that the treaties between the United States and the Cherokees should be kept. Georgia could not make the Indians follow its state laws. But Jackson did not listen to the court. He wanted to make the Cherokees live under Georgia's laws. He made the Cherokees sign a new treaty. It said that the Cherokees had to move west.

The Trail of Tears, painting by Robert Ottokar Lindneux, 1871–1970

Some Cherokees signed Jackson's treaty. But the Cherokee chief did not agree with the treaty. He and most of the Cherokees would not leave. The US army came to make them move. The Cherokees had to move to the Indian Territory, now called Oklahoma. The move was very hard for the Cherokees. Thousands died. Many died from the cold or from illness. The path the Cherokees traveled was called the **Trail of Tears**.

Where were the Cherokee Indians forced to move to?

Bank of the United States

Andrew Jackson did not like banks. He thought banks only helped the rich grow richer and more powerful. He thought banks gave little help to the common man. He also thought the national bank was against the law.

Jackson wanted to shut down the Bank of the United States. He told his secretary of the treasury to take all government money out of the bank. But the secretary said this would break the law. Jackson fired him. Then Jackson hired a man who worked to do what Jackson wanted.

Second Bank of the United States, Philadelphia, PA

Whigs and Democrats

Some people were not happy with Jackson's plans for the country. The Democratic-Republicans separated into two groups. A new political party formed. It was called the **Whig** Party. The Whigs thought Andrew Jackson was taking too much power. *Whig* was a name given to someone who did not like kings or presidents taking too much power. The other Democratic-Republicans changed their name to the **Democrats**. The United States now had two political parties again.

American Political Parties (1790s–1850s)

- Democratic-Republicans
- Federalists
- Democratic-Republicans
  - Democrats
  - Whigs

Tariffs

John C. Calhoun from South Carolina brought up a problem. Many years earlier, he supported a tariff to protect American manufacturers. But by 1828, Calhoun did not think the nation needed high tariffs anymore. American manufacturers were no longer being hurt by British imports. Instead, the Tariff of 1828 was hurting the people of South Carolina.

John C. Calhoun

Calhoun thought it was wrong to use a tariff to help only one part of the country, especially if the tariff hurt other parts of the country. He said this kind of law was against the Constitution.

Congress passed a new tariff in 1832. It fixed many problems. The new tariff pleased most of the southern states. But South Carolina was not pleased.

Calhoun said that a state could disobey a law if the law was against the Constitution. South Carolina leaders met to talk about the tariff. They said it was against the Constitution. They would not obey it.

Jackson said no state could declare a law against the Constitution. States must obey Congress's laws. He told South Carolina to pay the tariff. If South Carolina did not, Jackson would send soldiers to collect the money.

Calhoun did not want South Carolina to have to pay the tariff. Senator Henry Clay worked with Calhoun on a new tariff. It dropped the amount people had to pay. Everybody agreed to it. The tariff problem was solved for now.

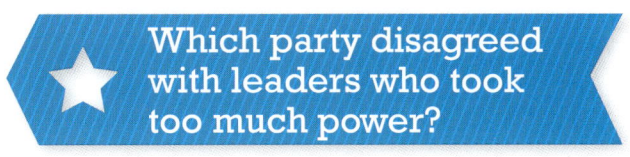

Which party disagreed with leaders who took too much power?

Abolitionists

After two terms as president, Jackson was ready to go home. Jackson was still well liked by the people. In 1837 his vice president **Martin Van Buren** became the eighth president of the United States. Van Buren had helped Jackson become president. Van Buren's hard work paid off, and now he was president. But he faced many problems as president. Hard times came. People lost their jobs. He was blamed for many of the problems in the country.

The Hermitage, home of Andrew Jackson from 1804–1845, Nashville, Tennessee

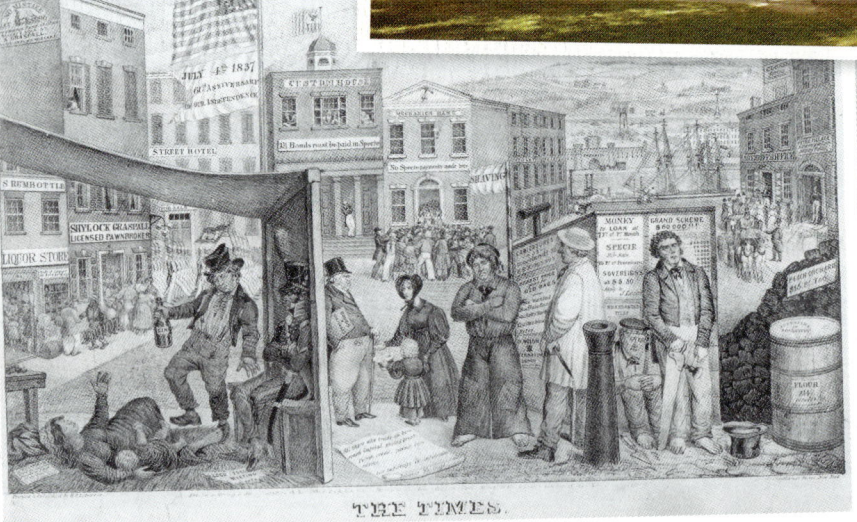

A picture of the Panic of 1837, a hard time in America. Many did not have money or jobs.

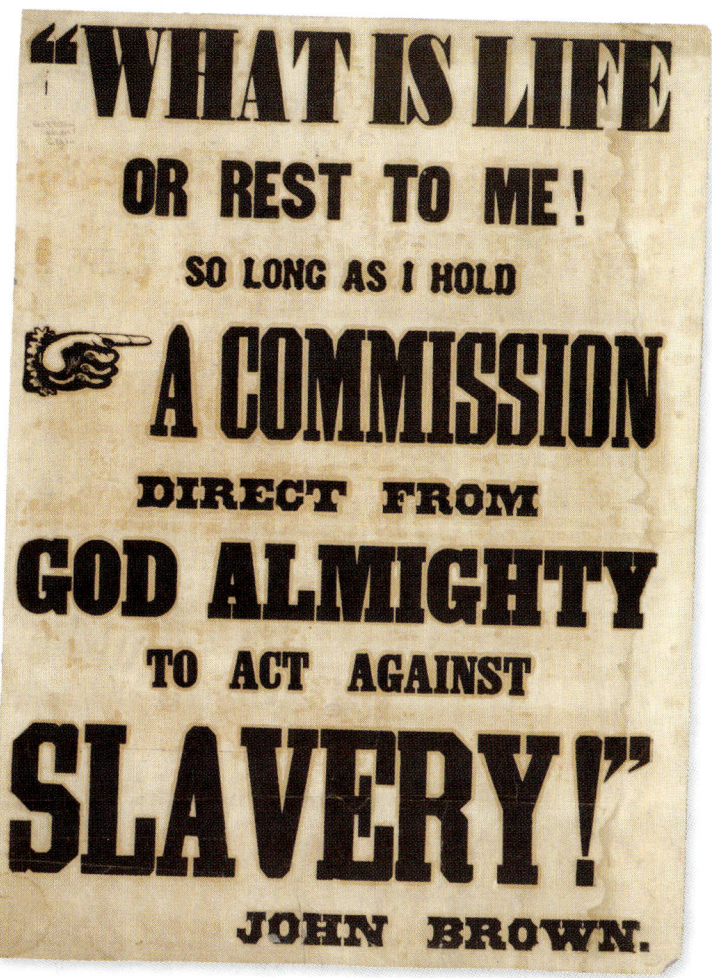

John Brown, an abolitionist, said nothing would stop him from fighting against slavery.

Slavery was one of the problems Van Buren faced. A small group of people called *abolitionists* wanted to end slavery right away. They wrote and sent writings to people around the country. People in the South did not like these writings. Postmasters in the South would not deliver mail from the abolitionists.

Abolitionist petition in a New York newspaper, 1836

The abolitionists found another way to get their news to the people. Abolitionists sent petitions to Congress. A **petition** is a written request for a right from a leader. The Bill of Rights said that the people had the right to send petitions to Congress.

John Quincy Adams now worked in Congress. He made sure the abolitionists' petitions were heard by Congress. The newspapers wrote about the petitions. Many people heard about how slavery was wrong.

Even today, American people still enjoy the freedoms that the Bill of Rights gives, such as the freedoms of religion and of speech.

While Van Buren was president something happened that showed people how wrong slavery was. A Spanish ship called the *Amistad* arrived on the coast of New York. African slaves had taken control of the ship. They hoped to sail to freedom. But the Spanish government demanded that the slaves be returned to their owners. Van Buren wanted to return the slaves. He did not support slave rebellions. He wanted to keep the votes of the southern states.

Abolitionists hired lawyers to help the slaves. The lawyers proved that the slaves had been kidnapped and sold under Spanish law. The case went to the Supreme Court. John Quincy Adams took the case before the Supreme Court. The Supreme Court ruled, or decided, that the Africans should be set free.

The African Missionary Association in America raised money to help send the Africans home. Five missionaries went with the freed slaves. Two of the missionaries were black Americans.

The *Amistad*

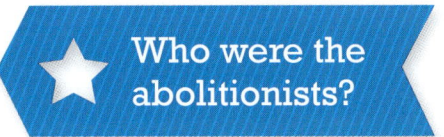

Who were the abolitionists?

7 Growth in the East

Focus

Because of inventions and immigration, the eastern United States experienced much growth.

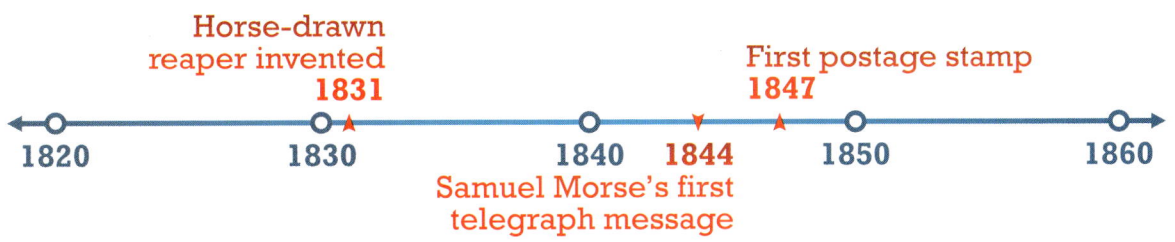

Canals, Steamboats, and Railroads

Canals

The United States was a growing nation. The amount of land grew. The number of people grew. The amount of money grew. All this growth brought the need to connect people. Boats traveled on canals to move goods and carry people around the nation. As the nation grew, it built more canals. By 1860, canals connected many states to the Mississippi River or the Atlantic Ocean.

Farmers earned money by selling their crops to distant cities. Farmers also bought cheaper goods from those cities. Cities grew beside the canals. People moving west lived and worked in these cities. As more canals were built, transporting goods became cheaper.

More goods could travel on rivers because of steamboats. People started steamboat companies to earn money. The number of companies grew. Each steamboat company wanted the most business. A company sometimes lowered its prices. This way more people might use that company's steamboats.

America had many people. The nation was growing. The people needed many goods. Businesses needed a large supply because there was much demand. **Supply** is the amount of goods that a business, or company, produces. Supply can come from farms, ranches, or factories. Supply also includes the services a business offers. **Demand** is the amount of goods and services that people want to buy. The more people buy goods and services, the higher the demand.

Steamboats

Thomas Gibbons owned a steamboat company. He ran his steamboats from New Jersey to different places. Gibbons faced a problem with one place. He could not run his steamboats to New York. Its leaders had given that right to Robert Fulton, another steamboat company owner.

Gibbons said that New York could not make rules like this. He took his case to the Supreme Court. Gibbons won the case. Now any steamboat could travel in New York waters.

Soon after this decision, a man named Cornelius Vanderbilt started his own steamboat company. He charged only one dollar for a person to ride his steamboat. Other steamboat companies charged three dollars for each person. Many companies dropped their prices. Then the supply and demand rose. Transportation of people and goods across the United States became cheaper.

The *Constitution*, a Hudson River steamboat

Railroads

In the 1830s, steamboat companies had new competition. Railroad companies began to lay more tracks. Railroads became a new way to move people and goods around the nation. Steamboats could only travel where a river went. But railroad tracks let trains travel to places where there were no rivers. Railroad tracks also connected cities across the country. Railroads brought more business to cities.

At first, using canals and rivers to transport goods was cheaper than using railroads. That soon changed. Trains became faster than ships. A ship could take three weeks to make a trip. But a train could make that trip in only four days.

The Stourbridge Lion, built in 1828, was America's first steam-powered locomotive (a vehicle that pulls trains).

Railroads brought the nation many benefits. Railroads helped news to travel more quickly. More goods from the East could be sold in the West. People looking for work used the railroad to travel where their skills were needed. People also began to travel to see other parts of the country. Canals, steamboats, and railroads helped connect the people in the United States.

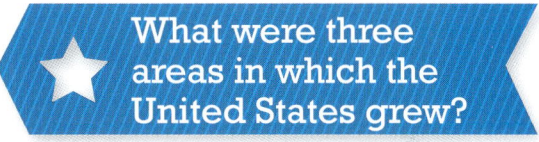
What were three areas in which the United States grew?

Early Canals & Railroads

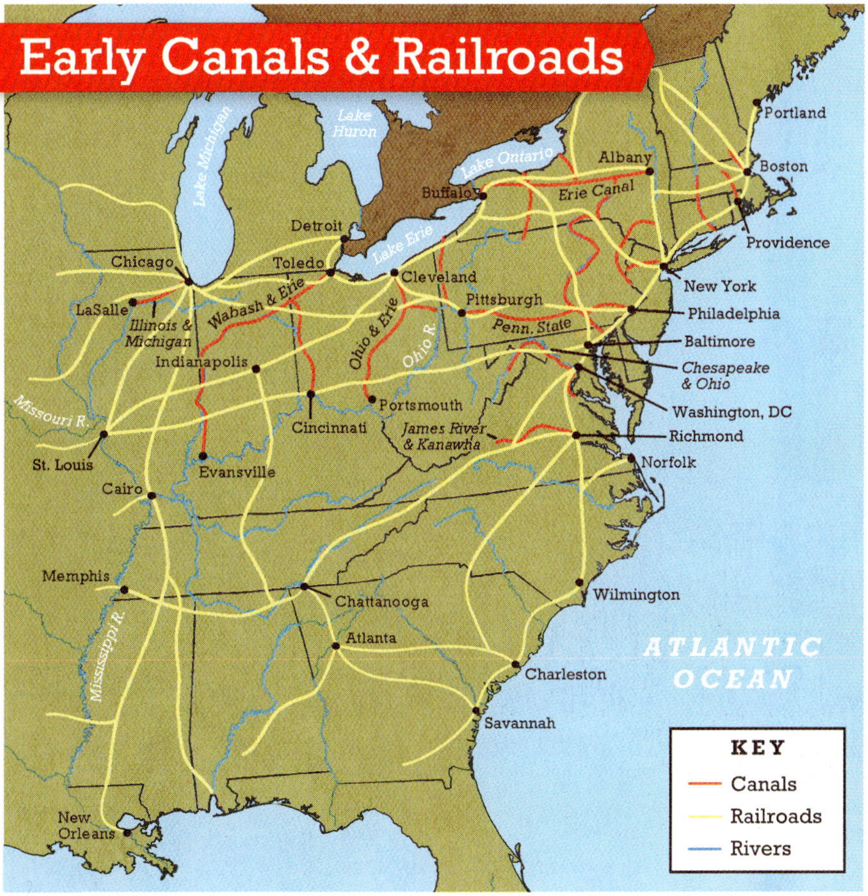

Changes for Cities and Farms

Cities in the North

Cities grew as the United States became more connected by steamboats and railroads. It became easy for boats and trains to transport goods. Cities became important for trade and opportunity.

The growth of cities led to problems. Cities had more crime. They needed police forces. Fires were also a threat in cities. Volunteer fire companies formed to put out fires.

Cities, however, had many benefits. Cities offered new kinds of jobs. People there often made more money than those who worked in rural areas. Often, people in cities could buy nicer things. City people also enjoyed parades, plays, and other activities.

Farms in the North

As cities grew, farms became more important. Farmers first grew food mainly for their families. By the 1850s that had changed. Farms produced extra food to sell to the growing cities. Farmers grew wheat, hay, and fruit trees. They raised chickens, hogs, and cattle. They often sold extra farm goods like butter and eggs. Canals and railroads helped take these goods to the cities.

Farmers enjoyed more success. They could work faster and better because of machines. Most farmers tried to improve their farms. They learned the latest ideas through farming newspapers and journals. Farmers used manufactured iron plows that were stronger and better than handmade plows. Inventors designed machines for mowing hay and threshing wheat. To **thresh** means to separate grain from its husks. These machines helped make farmers' work easier at harvest time.

Farms in the South

In the South farming was the main way people made a living. Most ran small farms. These farmers grew all their food and provided for the needs of their family. Some farmers also grew cotton or tobacco to sell.

The more successful farmers bought more land and more slaves. These farmers were called planters. Their large farms were called **plantations**. Most planters grew cotton as their main crop. Planters also grew sugarcane. Planting and harvesting crops was hard work. Many workers were needed. Planters believed they needed slaves in order to have successful plantations.

Southern Jobs and Cities

The South had many job opportunities other than farming. Some people worked in manufacturing businesses. Doctors, bankers, and shopkeepers lived and worked in the cities and towns. Blacksmiths made and fixed metal tools such as plows.

Some slaves worked in businesses. They served customers, worked as carpenters, or drove wagons. Some slaves worked in factories. Not all black people were slaves. Some worked as farmers. Others had different jobs in the cities. Free black Americans could own property and travel. But they were not treated equally with white Americans.

The South had several important port cities, such as Charleston, Savannah, and New Orleans. A **port** is a place near a body of water where ships dock to load and unload goods. Port cities in the South were important for shipping cotton north or across the ocean. Port cities provided many job opportunities.

What was the main way people in the South made their living?

Factories, Inventions & Patents

Factories

Most businesses in the Northeast were manufacturers. The Northeast had many rivers. At first, factories needed to be next to rivers. The power of a flowing river turned water wheels. These wheels gave power for machines. Since farming was hard in the Northeast, many people worked in factories.

In the 1830s and 1840s, factories began to use steam engines for power. Factories no longer needed rivers for power. Other parts of the country began to build their own factories.

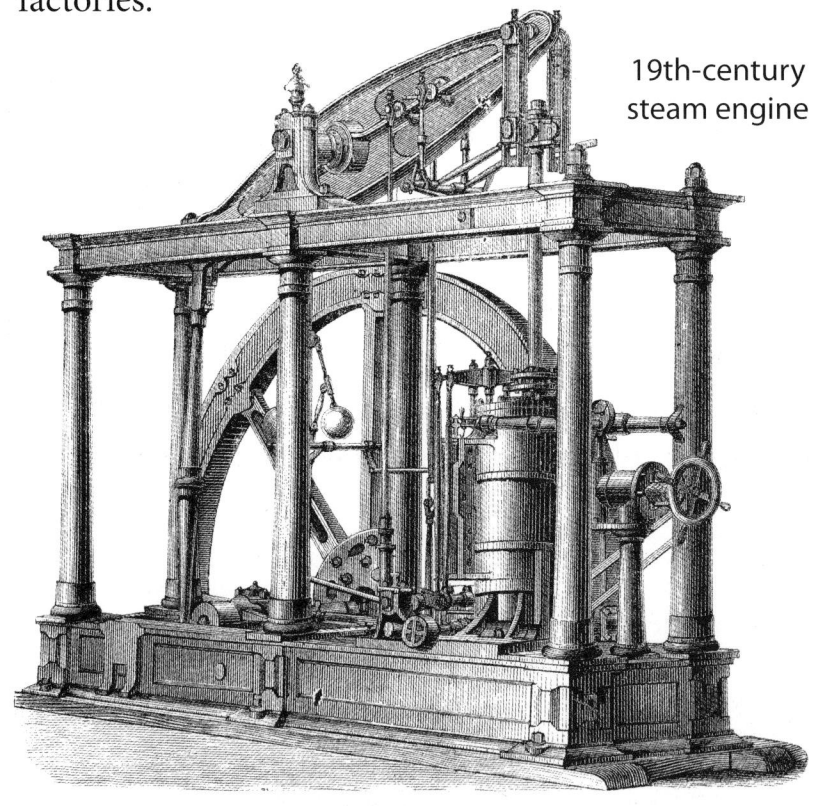

19th-century steam engine

Inventions

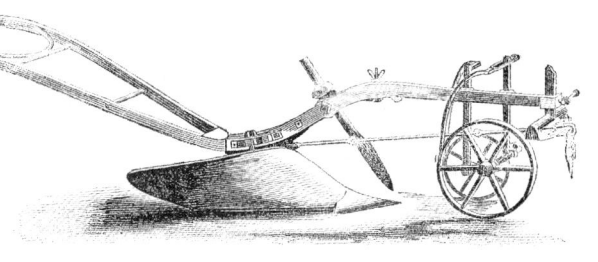
plow

Inventors made new things or improved old ones. Obed Hussey and **Cyrus McCormick** invented reapers in the early 1830s. A **reaper** cuts and gathers grain. McCormick improved his reaper. It became a useful and common tool among farmers. Later in the 1830s John Deere made a steel plow. Soil stuck to iron plows. Farmers had to stop and clean them often. Soil did not stick to Deere's plow because it was made of steel.

shoemaker's sewing machine

Also in the 1830s rubber became popular in America. People liked the idea of waterproof rubber boots and coats. But in cold weather the rubber became hard and cracked. In hot weather it became sticky like glue. Charles Goodyear discovered a way to make better rubber that did not have these problems.

In the 1840s Elias Howe invented the sewing machine. This machine sewed faster than several people sewing by hand.

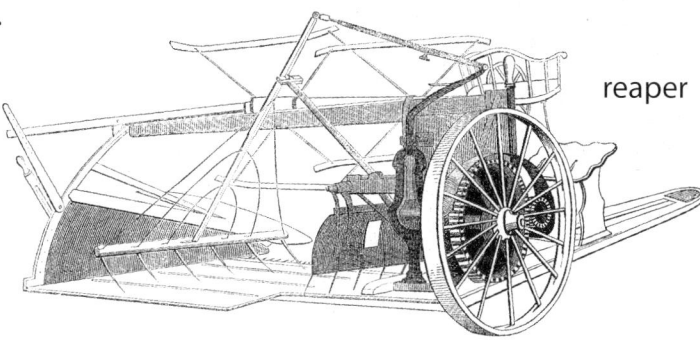
reaper

171

Patents

Most inventors wanted to make money from their work. People like Charles Goodyear worked many years to come up with the right way to make a product. But if anyone could copy an inventor's work, anyone could make money from it. The inventor would make little money. He would not be able to keep inventing.

To help inventors, the US government gave them patents. A **patent** is a right that says only the inventor may make or sell his invention. Because of patents, inventors could earn money from their inventions. Inventors could keep working on new inventions. The Patent Office, which gave patents to inventors, became busy in the 1830s.

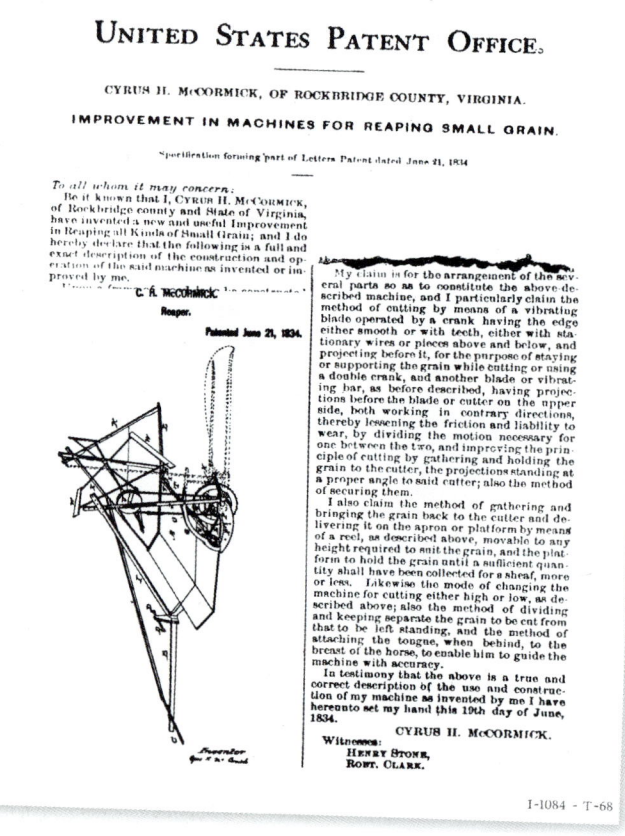

Cyrus McCormick's reaper patent, 1834

What helped inventors make money from their inventions?

Immigrants

Many changes happened in the United States from the 1820s through the 1850s. One of the biggest changes was the growing number of immigrants. An **immigrant** is a person who comes to live in a country from somewhere else. Many people from Europe came to the United States during this time.

By 1860 many immigrants had settled in the North. Immigrants from the same country often settled in the same area. Many immigrants from Holland settled in Michigan. Those from Norway and Sweden often settled in Wisconsin and Minnesota. Irish immigrants often stayed in the cities of New York and Boston.

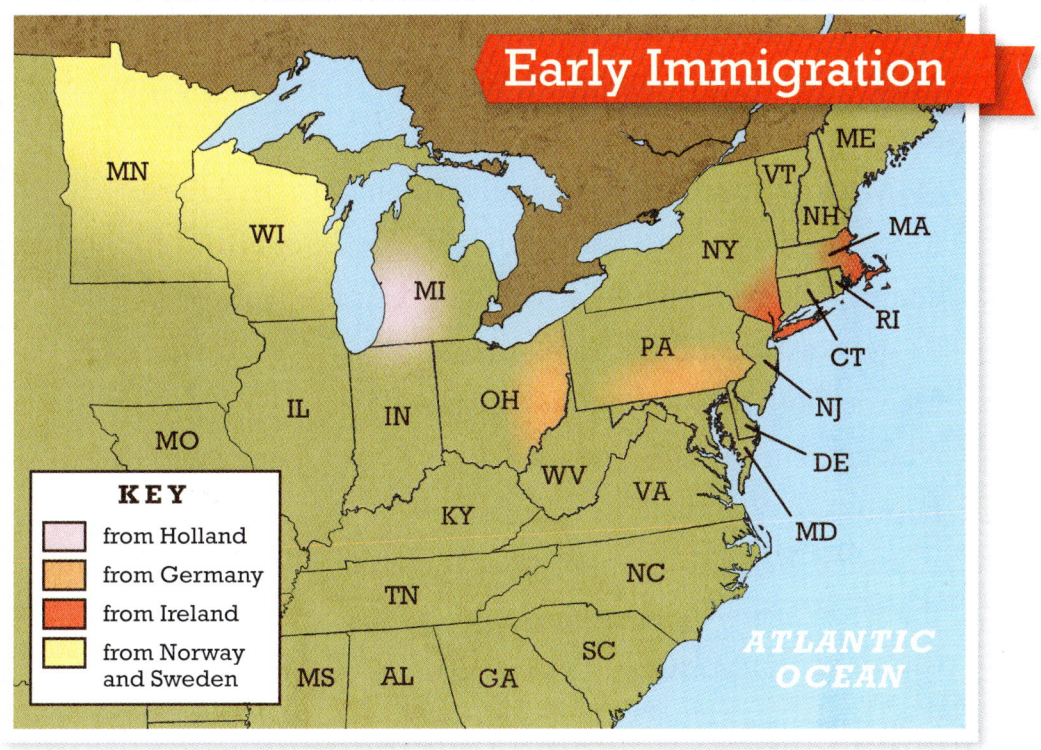

Early Immigration

173

Most immigrants during this time were Irish or German. Many people in Ireland were poor. More than one million people had died of hunger. Irish people came to the United States looking for a new life.

Many Irish immigrants found life in America hard. Most came with little money. They could not afford to buy a farm or start a business. Many of the men worked as canal diggers or road builders. Women worked in factories. Still, life was better than what people faced back home. The Irish who came to America wrote letters home. They encouraged family and friends to join them.

Some German immigrants came with more money than the Irish. Many German immigrants bought farms. They settled in the Midwest. Groups of families bought farms near one another and started farming communities.

Americans did not always trust the immigrants. They were afraid the immigrants would change the American way of life. They were concerned that the immigrants would stay in their own areas and not become Americans.

People also worried about the immigrants' beliefs about God. Many immigrants had different beliefs than most Americans. People feared that immigrants would change what it meant to be American.

Members of the Know-Nothing Party did not like most immigration.

The immigrants did change the United States. They brought their cultures and traditions with them. There were both good and bad changes. But America also changed the immigrants. Few spoke English when they first came. But their children quickly learned to speak English. Immigrants began to accept American values. They developed a love for freedom and democracy. Immigrants became part of the American way of life.

What countries were most of the immigrants to America from?

New Ways to Communicate
The United States Post Office

The United States was a larger nation than most European nations. People in America wanted to communicate across their large land. **Communicate** means to share information. One way people communicate is by writing letters.

Congress was in charge of the post office. By the 1820s, more people worked for the United States Post Office than for any other part of the national government. Almost every town had its own post office. Post offices delivered letters across the country. Post offices also brought news about other places.

As transportation improved, so did mail delivery. The post office used steamboats and trains to take the mail across the country. Changes in transportation helped letters and news travel faster.

The US Postal Service

Soon news had a faster way to travel than by mail. **Samuel Morse** invented the telegraph. The **telegraph** was a machine that used a wire to send messages. Morse's telegraph sent pulses of electricity over a wire strung on poles. The pulses caused long or short marks on a piece of paper. Then a telegraph worker would change these marks to letters.

Samuel Morse

What: inventor
When: 1791–1872
Where: United States

Samuel Morse was an inventor and an accomplished painter. One time his wife was very sick. But Morse received this news too late. He was not able to see her before she died. This event caused Morse to invent the electrical telegraph. It became valuable, and he made a small fortune from it. He spent the end of his life using his money to help others.

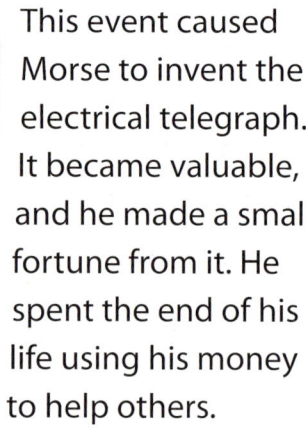

In 1844, Morse was in Washington, DC. He used the telegraph to send a message to his helper in Baltimore, Maryland. The message read: "WHAT HATH GOD WROUGHT." The phrase came from Numbers 23:23 in the Bible. Morse chose this first message because he believed God helped him invent the telegraph.

Morse's telegraph changed communication. News now traveled in an instant. Morse wanted the government to buy his telegraph. The government did not buy it. But many people wanted to use Morse's telegraph. Businesses put up telegraph lines across the nation. Newspapers used the telegraph to spread news quickly across the country. Bankers used the news to make decisions about their money.

Since the telegraph, other inventors have made and improved machines of communication. However, people still remember the telegraph. It was the first invention that made it possible for people to quickly get news from far away.

Improvements in Communication

letter carrier

telegraph

fax

e-mail

What improved when transportation improved?

Christians in the Growing Nation

Mail on Sundays

More churches were built as the nation grew larger. Pastors and missionaries moved to the West. Preachers taught people to put their trust in God. In the 1800s most people believed in God.

Sometimes people did not agree about how things should be. The post office delivered mail seven days a week. This caused a problem on Sunday. Mail carriages were noisy. Sometimes this noise bothered the people at church. Some believed the Bible taught that people should not work on Sundays. Many Christians wanted the post office to be closed on Sundays.

Christians never decided on a solution about the Sunday mail. But the invention of the telegraph helped. Mail was delivered less often on Sundays.

Reforms

All the improvements in America excited people. New inventions, better transportation, and faster communication made life better for many.

Some Americans wanted the country to improve morally as well. Many worked in voluntary societies to make the nation better. People wanted reforms to make Americans more moral. A **reform** is a change to make something better or more just. Volunteers, or people who work without pay, helped with the reforms. One attempt for reform was the **temperance movement**. Its volunteers wanted people not to get drunk. People who got drunk often hurt themselves and others. Sometimes these drinkers spent all their money on drinks like beer and whiskey. Then they had no money left to buy food. Some people lost their jobs for being drunk.

Many immigrants ate and drank at beer gardens, businesses that served beer.

At first, volunteers of the temperance movement wanted to stop people from getting drunk. But many people found it hard to stop getting drunk. The volunteers decided to change their plan. Instead of telling people to drink less beer, volunteers said people should not drink beer or whiskey at all. The volunteers wanted people to live better and healthier lives. Volunteers said that people should stop buying or selling beer and whiskey. Doing this would help others and show love for them.

Temperance movement poster

The temperance movement was just one of many reforms. Some reforms tried to end slavery, improve education, and improve prisons.

Most Americans wanted their country to get better. Although the reforms had good results, some Christians felt they were not enough. The reforms helped many people. But some volunteers did not believe that a person needed God's grace to change. Some of them did not like the Bible's teaching that every person is a sinner from birth. They thought that a person could change if he made up his mind to do so.

Many Christians were concerned that reforms only changed people's behavior. Jesus said that what was in a person's heart mattered as much as his actions. These Christians were glad to see the reforms happen. But they knew real change could only come through God's grace. Christians agreed that the reforms were important. They were glad to see children getting a better education. They were glad that fewer people were getting drunk. But knowing God rightly is most important. Reforms can only help people if they know God rightly.

How did reform movements help make America better?

Making a quilt

A quilt is made of two layers of cloth sewn together with a padding of cotton, feathers, or other material between. A quilt is made from blocks of fabric with the same or different patterns. Machines made fabric easier to make. So fabric became more affordable. The sewing machine made it easier to make quilts.

Learning Lessons from Progress

The 1820s to the 1850s were years of amazing progress, or improvement, for the United States. Steamboats, railroads, and the telegraph connected people who were far apart. Inventions helped people work faster and produce more goods.

The inventions of the 1800s improved lives. Farmers used better plows and improved reapers to grow more food. These crops helped to feed the nation. Better and faster transportation brought the food into the growing cities. Easier and faster communication brought the growing nation closer together.

Inventors used their God-given gifts to improve life for many others. Several inventors gave God the credit for their skills. To this day Americans celebrate their inventors.

Progress also brought problems. Better transportation made life busier. Being able to travel meant less time for being still and thinking. The telegraph and the mail delivery gave people more information than ever before. But more information does not always make people wiser. Sometimes more information makes people forget the wisdom from the past.

Progress has changed people's way of life in many ways. People have learned to use many new inventions. People should use the gift of progress wisely and for God's purposes.

 What changes did progress bring to America?

8 The United States Spreads West

Focus

Some Americans believed they were supposed to settle the western parts of North America.

Texas Gains Independence

Americans began to settle the land west of the Mississippi River. President Thomas Jefferson had paid for the land. Some of this land was near land that belonged to Mexico.

In 1821 Mexico became free from Spain. By 1824 Mexico had its own constitution. The new Mexican government wanted people to settle in Mexico's northern areas. One of these areas was Texas. The Mexican government sold land at low prices, wanting Americans to move there.

US and Mexico

The Mexicans made laws for the Americans who moved to Mexico. The Americans had to obey these laws. They had to become Catholics. They had to free their slaves. The Mexicans wanted the Americans to become Mexicans. But many Americans did not keep these laws.

The Mexican Constitution of 1824 allowed Texas and other parts of Mexico to govern themselves. But things changed in 1833. A general in the Mexican army became the president of Mexico. His name was **Santa Anna**. He got rid of the constitution. He made new laws that gave more power to the Mexican government. He sent soldiers to make people obey the new laws. Many did not like this. They were worried that Santa Anna would make them obey laws about slavery and religion.

People in Texas decided to fight against Santa Anna. The Texans would fight to bring back the Mexican Constitution of 1824. It had given them more freedom. People in the United States heard about the fighting in Texas. Many Americans near Texas wanted to help this fight for freedom. They crossed the border to help the Texan army.

In Texas there was an old mission, or church, called the Alamo. Soldiers had used it as a fort in the past. Some Texans and Americans decided to do the same. About two hundred men stayed at the Alamo. They sent a messenger to bring back more Texan soldiers. But they never came. Santa Anna and his large army came. They defeated the men at the Alamo. Santa Anna ordered all the prisoners that were taken in the battle to be killed. Then he went to the town of Goliad. There he defeated more Texan soldiers. He again killed most of his prisoners. Only a few escaped.

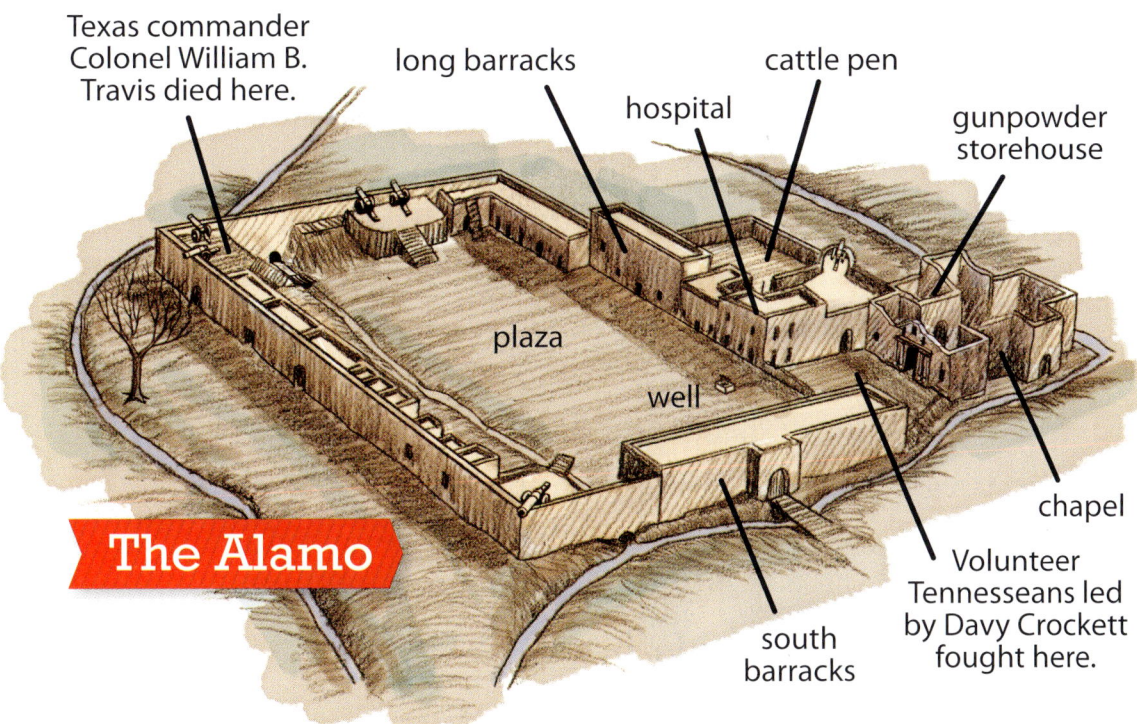

The Alamo

The Texans seemed to be losing. The commander of the Texan army was Sam Houston. He surprised Santa Anna in the Battle of San Jacinto. Houston attacked when Santa Anna was not expecting it. Houston's soldiers charged. They yelled, "Remember the Alamo!" Santa Anna was finally defeated and captured.

Santa Anna

The Texans changed their goal for fighting. They were no longer just fighting to bring back the Mexican Constitution of 1824. They wanted to be free from Mexico. They wanted to be their own country. Sam Houston told Santa Anna that he and his army could go free. But Santa Anna had to agree to free Texas from Mexico. Santa Anna agreed. Texas became independent on March 2, 1836.

Texans elected **Sam Houston** as the president of their new nation. What next? Would Texas stay independent? Or would it join with the United States? America had thirteen free states and thirteen slave states. President Jackson knew that adding a new state would cause trouble. The number of states would no longer be even. Texas was not added as a state. It remained an independent nation for nine years.

What happened at the Alamo?

Americans Move West

Oregon Country

During the 1830s, Americans also moved west across the Great Plains. They began to settle in an area called Oregon Country. Missionaries led the way. Christians wanted to spread the gospel to the Indians there.

Missionaries **Marcus and Narcissa Whitman** traveled to Oregon Country in 1836. The Whitmans packed too many things in their covered wagon. It was too heavy for the animals to pull. So the Whitmans had to leave many of their things by the side of the trail.

Many traveled west on the Oregon Trail. The Whitmans founded a mission settlement and gave care and supplies to travelers on the trail.

The Whitmans finally arrived in Oregon Country. They built a mission for the Cayuse Indians. It was in a beautiful valley. Many pioneers also stopped at the mission. A **pioneer** is a person who is the first to settle an area. Some pioneers traveled for at least six months and ran out of supplies. The Whitmans had a farm. It supplied food for these pioneers. The Whitmans also set up a school for both Indian and pioneer children.

Marcus Whitman

Marcus Whitman was a doctor for the Cayuse people and the pioneers. But the Cayuse people did not welcome the Whitmans. The Cayuse did not like pioneers coming to their lands. One time a sickness spread through the Cayuse tribe. Many people died. The Cayuse believed Marcus Whitman's medicine had poisoned them. This upset the Cayuse. In anger, they killed the Whitmans and twelve settlers at the mission house.

Narcissa Whitman

Eliza Spalding

What: missionary
When: 1807–1851
Where: Oregon Country
Eliza Spalding and her husband lived with the Nez Perce Indians. Mrs. Spalding drew pictures for her husband's Bible lessons. She also taught the Nez Perce practical skills, such as spinning and knitting. Eliza Spalding lived a life of Christian service.

Henry and Eliza Spalding also went to Oregon Country as missionaries. They built a mission to the Nez Perce Indians. It was in a rugged mountain area. The Spaldings wrote Christian writings and songs in the Nez Perce language. They started a school and began a church. Some Nez Perce people trusted Christ.

But the US Army told the Spaldings to leave Oregon Country. It was too dangerous. The Whitmans had died because of trouble with the Indians. The Spaldings left. But Henry Spalding returned almost twenty-five years later. Many Nez Perce Indians trusted Christ. Later, the Nez Perce people spread the gospel to other Indian peoples.

Mormons Move to Utah

Another group of people traveled west. They wanted to practice their beliefs. They were called **Mormons**. They settled in Illinois. Their leader was **Joseph Smith**.

Smith did not want everyone to know what he taught. He knew many Americans would be shocked by his teachings. A local newspaper printed an article about him. It said that Smith taught that men could have more than one wife. It also said Smith believed in more than one god. Smith's teachings worried many people. They did not think his ideas were good.

Smith had his followers destroy the newspaper's printing press. Smith was arrested and put in jail. Later, Smith was killed by a mob of people who did not like his teachings.

Brigham Young became the new Mormon leader. He planned a way for the Mormons to move further west. He led them to the region of the **Great Salt Lake** in Utah. He thought that no one else would want to settle there. The Mormons would then be free to practice their beliefs. But other Americans moved further west too. They were concerned about what the Mormons taught. Religion should not be an excuse for doing wrong.

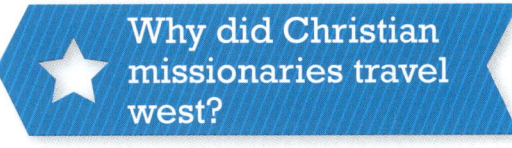

Why did Christian missionaries travel west?

Activity

Examining a covered wagon

The covered wagon was sometimes called a prairie schooner. From a distance it looked like a ship's sails.
How big was a covered wagon? What could fit in it?

Three Presidents

William Henry Harrison

In the election of 1840, the Whig Party knew they had a good chance of winning against the Democrats. President Martin Van Buren was a Democrat. He faced many problems while in office. So the Whigs knew the Americans might not want the Democrats in power again.

William Henry Harrison was a Whig and a popular general. He had won several battles against the British. Later he was a governor. He had also served in the US Congress.

Harrison ran to be the next president. He chose John Tyler to run as vice president. Harrison won the election and became president after Van Buren. But the Whig success did not last. President Harrison died one month later. **William Henry Harrison** had been the oldest US president elected up to that time. And he was the first US president to die while in office.

John Tyler

When a president dies, the vice president becomes the next president. After Harrison died, John Tyler became the next president. Like Harrison, Tyler was also a Whig. But Tyler did not always agree with the Whigs.

Tyler agreed more with the Democrats. The Whigs did not like this. They decided to remove him from the Whig party. Tyler then removed some Whigs from their jobs. They had been working in the national government. He replaced them with Democrats. Tyler also tried to add Texas as a state.

James K. Polk

In 1844 the Whigs chose Henry Clay to run for president, and the Democrats chose James K. Polk. Polk wanted to increase the borders of the United States. He and many Americans wanted to add Texas as a state. The election between Clay and Polk was close, but Polk won.

Some Whigs and most Democrats in Congress voted to add Texas as a state of the United States.

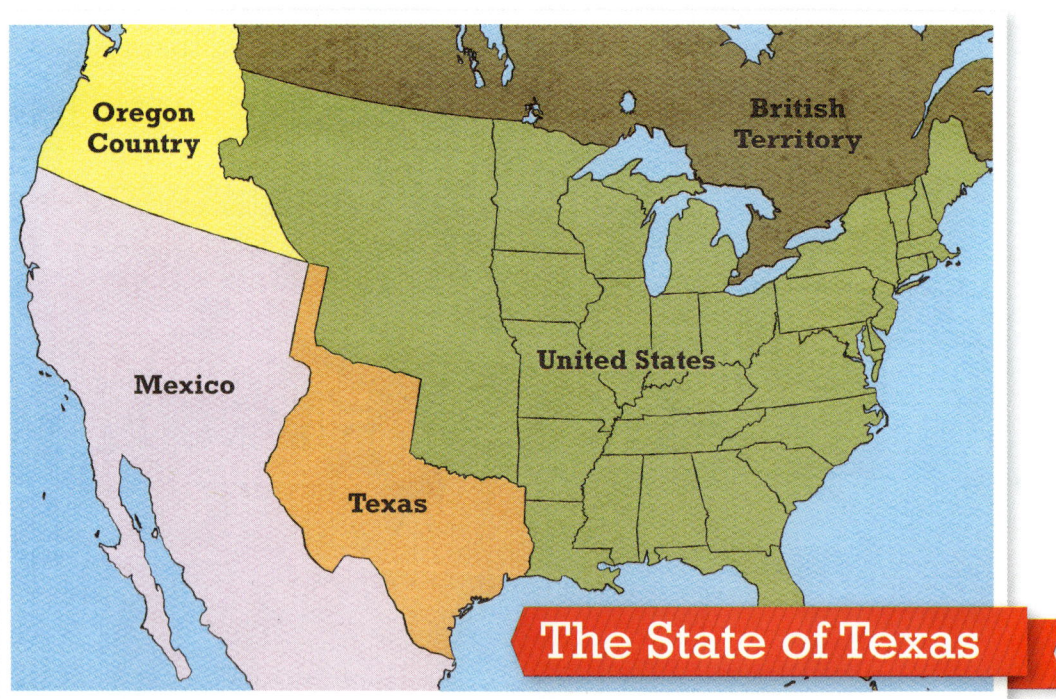

The State of Texas

Toward the Pacific

Americans continued to move west across North America. Many Americans believed that all the land in the west should belong to them. President Polk liked the idea of more land. He believed America would be stronger if it had more land.

Oregon Country

The Oregon Country was a large area of land in the west. The Americans and the British shared this land. The British used it for fur trade. Americans used the land to build farms.

By the 1840s the Democrats thought that all of Oregon Country should belong to the Americans. One Democrat wrote a newspaper article. He said that God gave the United States the right to own the "whole of the Continent." This belief was called **Manifest Destiny**. It said that God gave Americans all the lands between the Atlantic and Pacific Oceans. The Bible does not teach this.

President James K. Polk

"It is confidently believed that our system may be safely extended to the utmost bounds of our territorial limits, and that as it shall be extended the bonds of our Union, so far from being weakened, will become stronger."

The British did not want to give up all of Oregon Country. But they did not want to start a war with the Americans. So in 1846 the British and the Americans made a treaty, or agreement. Each side would have a part of the Oregon Country. The border would be on the **49th parallel**. This is a line of latitude on the earth at 49° N (49 degrees north). The agreement allowed the British to keep Vancouver Island. And the Americans would let the British travel on the Columbia River that ran through the American side. Both nations liked the agreement.

Polk was glad to settle these matters. He had other matters to think about. The United States and Mexico were not getting along.

What was Manifest Destiny?

Westward Expansion

California

Polk wanted more land in the west. He wanted California and the land between California and Texas. Polk wanted California because it had excellent port cities. Port cities would give the United States a better way to the ocean.

Polk faced a problem. California belonged to Mexico. But Polk thought that California would be easy to take from Mexico. Most Mexicans lived far away from California. And Mexico could not afford to keep a large army in California.

Landing of the American forces under
General Winfield Scott at Vera Cruz, 1847

In 1845 Polk told the US Navy to get ready for war. Polk ordered the navy to be ready to capture one of the port cities in California. At the same time, Polk sent an army to California. John C. Frémont led this army. They tricked the Mexicans by pretending to be explorers and mapmakers. But Frémont and his army were really there to fight a war.

Polk also sent a man to talk with the leaders of Mexico. They talked about buying California and other land. But the Mexicans did not want to sell any land. They believed America had been wrong to take Texas from them. They also did not agree with the Americans over the southern border of Texas. The Mexicans did not want to talk about selling their land.

Mexican-American War

By early 1846 President Polk learned that Mexico did not want to sell land to the United States. He then sent US troops to a river called the Rio Grande. It flowed between Texas and Mexico. Both the United States and Mexico claimed land north of the river. Many in Congress feared a war with Mexico. They were upset that Polk sent troops near Mexico.

General Zachary Taylor led the US troops. He moved them to the river. A Mexican commander told Taylor to leave. Taylor did not leave. Instead, he blocked Mexican supplies that were coming up the river.

Battle of Chapultepec, 1847, Mexico City, Mexico

A month later the Mexicans crossed the river. They attacked the US troops. Polk asked Congress for a declaration of war. Many Americans were against this. But Congress still passed the declaration of war against Mexico. Some said that the way Polk had started the war was against the law.

Success in California

The United States and Mexico were now at war. Polk sent one part of the US Army to capture the Mexican city of Santa Fe. Another part of the army was already in California to capture it. Both groups were successful.

A stamp showing the capture of Santa Fe

Why was California important to Polk?

Battle of Buena Vista during the Mexican-American War. Art by Adolphe Jean-Baptiste Bayot, 1851, based on a drawing by Carl Nebel (1805–1855).

Success in Texas

General Taylor also had success as he moved south. Taylor and his men had an advantage. Their guns and cannons were better than the Mexican ones. Taylor kept moving his troops south into Mexico. He captured the Mexican city of Monterrey. This was an important victory.

Santa Anna still ruled a part of Mexico. He moved his large army north to meet Taylor. Both sides fought in the village of Buena Vista. The Mexicans had more soldiers. At first it seemed that the Mexicans would win the battle. But Taylor stood firm. The Americans pushed the Mexicans back. During the night, Santa Anna withdrew his army.

Mexican-American War

The United States was close to winning the war. Polk sent an army to Mexico's capital, Mexico City. The Mexican army had more soldiers. But the US Army had better leaders. Santa Anna blocked the road to Mexico City. He controlled a tall hill along the road. The American soldiers could not get to the capital.

An American soldier, Robert E. Lee, came up with a plan. There was another tall hill nearby. It was full of thorns. Santa Anna could not use that hill. But Lee found a way to move a cannon onto it. He and his men fired at Santa Anna's army and forced them off their hill. The US Army was then able to conquer Mexico City.

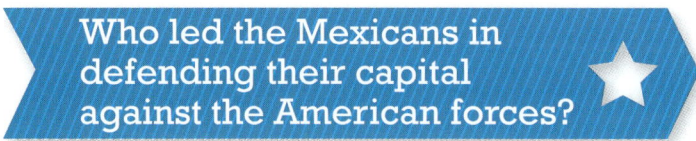

Who led the Mexicans in defending their capital against the American forces?

Results of the War

The United States had conquered the land Polk wanted. Polk now wanted the war with Mexico to be over. Some Americans did not like how Polk started the war. They thought the war was unjust. They thought it was the wrong way to get more land.

Many Christians feared God's judgment on America. Many in Congress had believed that the war's main purpose was to defend the border between Mexico and the United States. These Congress members thought America was wrong to take more land from Mexico.

James Alexander

James Alexander was a pastor and a teacher. He thought there was no good reason to fight the war. He said, "Never have I so much feared the judgments of God on us as a nation."

Polk said that Mexico owed land to the United States. He thought that Mexico should pay with land for the cost of the war. Polk tried to make the Mexicans sign a peace treaty quickly. He told them he would ask for more land if they took too long to sign a treaty.

Polk sent Nicholas Trist to make a treaty with Mexico. Polk wanted a large amount of land. The Mexicans refused his demands. So Polk demanded even more land.

But Trist did not make a treaty that gave Polk all the land he wanted. Instead, Trist asked Mexico for the least amount of land possible. He believed the United States had been wrong in the war. Polk was not happy. But the treaty gave him the land he had set out to gain for the United States.

General Zachary Taylor had a chance to become the next president. Taylor and his army had won many battles in the Mexican-American War. In 1848, Taylor won the election. He became the next president of the United States. He was part of the Whig Party, so the Whigs had a man in the White House once again.

Who did Polk send to make a treaty with Mexico?

The California Gold Rush

In 1848 the Mexicans signed the peace treaty that ended the Mexican-American War. Nine days before the treaty was signed, something exciting happened in California. Workers at a sawmill discovered gold. A man named John Sutter owned the land where the gold was found. He tried to keep it a secret. However, such news could not be kept secret for long. The news spread to the east. In **1849** many people rushed to California in search of gold. They were called **forty-niners**, named after the year of the gold rush.

People from all over the world went to California to look for gold. California's population grew quickly. Many wanted to get rich fast. But most miners did not get rich. A **miner** is a person who gets natural resources from the earth. Many did not find any gold. Some found gold but did not spend it wisely.

The merchants in California gained the most money from the gold rush. The forty-niners needed supplies. The merchants sold the miners food, clothes, shelter, and tools. Since the supply of goods was low, the prices of the goods became high.

James Marshall at Sutter's Mill in Coloma, California, about 1850

Mining towns sprang up in California. There were no local governments set up yet, so the people ruled by majority. In this way, each mining town was a democracy. People made their own decisions. But without government and laws, the towns became dangerous. Sometimes the town's strongest people ruled. Sometimes they ruled in a disorderly or violent way.

Some slave owners did not take their slaves to California. They feared that slaves would run away to mine for gold. Miners without slaves thought it was unfair for someone to use slaves to search for gold. It gave the slave owner help that others did not have. Miners without slaves pushed for California to be a free state.

Many people lived in California by now. Soon California applied to become a state. In 1850, California became part of the United States. California entered as a free state.

Portsmouth Square, San Francisco, California, 1851

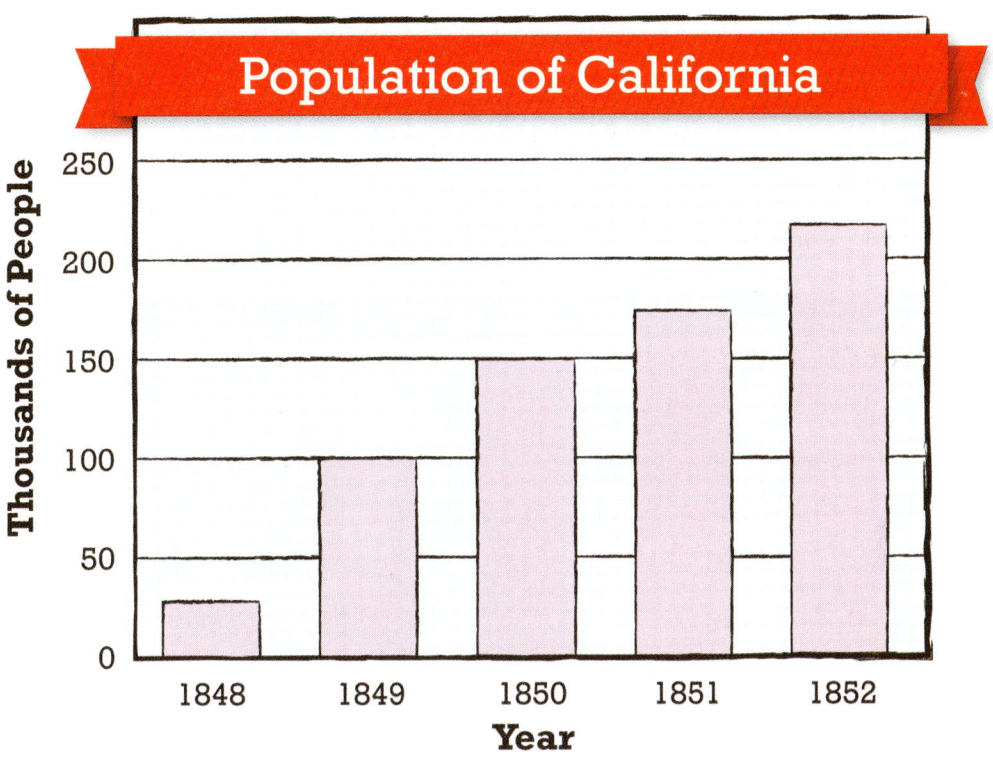

By 1850 the United States had spread across the entire continent of North America. Most people still lived east of the Mississippi River. But many were already moving west. Some Americans did not agree with the way President Polk had gained these new lands for the United States. But Mexico had already signed a treaty. The war was over. Americans had to decide how they were going to use these new lands. Gold had already been found in California. And new resources would be discovered in coming years.

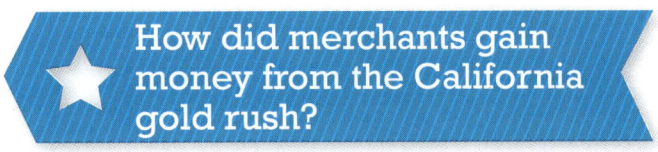

How did merchants gain money from the California gold rush?

9 A Nation Dividing

Focus
Slavery divided the United States so much that some southern states left the nation.

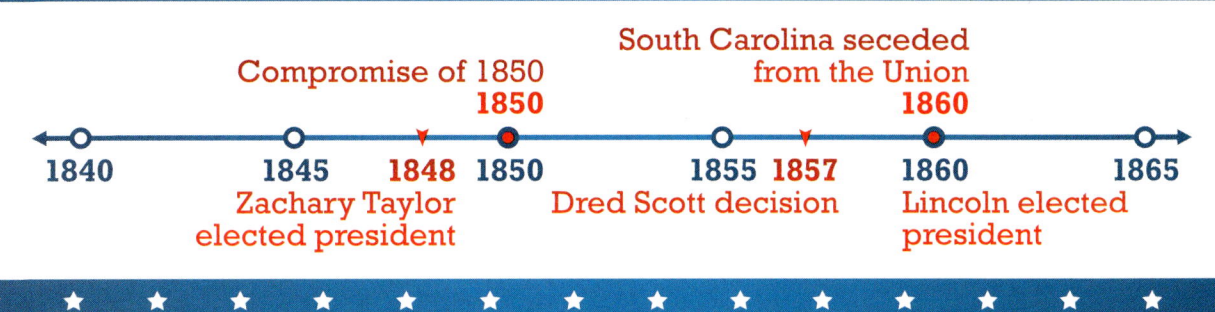

The Compromise of 1850

Winning the Mexican-American War gave the United States a new problem. The national government gained many new lands. Congress could not agree on whether or not to allow slavery in those lands. America elected General Zachary Taylor as the new president. Even though he owned slaves, he did not want slavery to spread. He said it should stay where it was.

John C. Calhoun had different ideas. He said the national government did not own the new lands. Calhoun believed that all the states owned these lands or territories together. Calhoun also believed that slaves were property. He said that a person could bring property into the territories. Calhoun said that Congress could not block slaves from the new lands.

Slave & Free States, 1850s

Senator Henry Clay thought of a way to fix the problem. He wrote a bill that gave everybody something that they wanted. California would be a free state. The other new territories could vote to be free or slave once they became states. Clay also wrote a bill that helped slave owners get back their runaway slaves.

Clay hoped that all states would like part of his plans. Each state got something it wanted. But President Taylor did not like the bill. He said it allowed slavery into the territories. The slave states also did not like the bill. They wanted California to be a slave state. Later, Clay became sick. He had to leave Congress. Others continued his work.

Stephen Douglas

Another senator, named Stephen Douglas, tried to get help for Clay's bill. Douglas split the bill into five bills. He was able to gain support from Congress. It voted to accept each part. These bills formed the Compromise of 1850.

Vice President Becomes President

President Taylor died during this time. The vice president became the next president. His name was Millard Fillmore. He did not like slavery, but he liked the new bills. Fillmore thought America needed a compromise to stay together. The slavery problem was dividing, or separating, the country. A compromise would help America set aside the problems of the new lands for a while. President Fillmore signed the bills once Congress passed them.

Millard Fillmore

Many Americans wanted to stop talking about slavery. People hoped the Compromise of 1850 would solve the problem. But people continued to disagree about slavery.

 What did the Compromise of 1850 decide about the spread of slavery?

215

The Problem of Runaway Slaves

Henry Brown

The Compromise of 1850 was supposed to settle the disagreement between the slave states and the free states. But one part of the compromise caused much trouble. One bill made people return runaway slaves. Many free states had laws to help people who did not want to return runaway slaves. But the Compromise of 1850 said free states had to return runaway slaves to slave owners.

A few slaves made daring escapes. One of these people was Henry "Box" Brown. Brown's first master was kind and treated his slaves well. But after that man died, a new master treated Brown badly. This master even sold Brown's two children. Brown wanted freedom and had an idea. He asked some friends to mail him in a box to the Anti-Slavery Society in Philadelphia. Brown's idea worked. When the box was opened in Philadelphia, he came out a free man.

Illustration of Henry "Box" Brown, 1849

Harriet Tubman

Slaves tried many ways to escape. Some fled to freedom on the Underground Railroad. It was not a real railroad. The **Underground Railroad** was a group of people who helped runaway slaves. The group provided safe places for slaves to hide on their way to freedom. In some places the Underground Railroad was well planned. People at one safe place could tell runaways where to find the next safe place. Often runaway slaves had to find their own way from one safe place to another.

Harriet Tubman

People who knew about the safe places and the best ways of escape were called **conductors**. Sometimes they led groups of enslaved people to freedom. One of the best-known conductors was Harriet Tubman. Although she was married to a free black man, her owner could still sell her away from her husband. Tubman ran away to freedom after her owner began to sell his slaves. She hoped that her husband would follow her to a free state.

Tubman went back to slave states many times to rescue slaves. People called her Moses because she freed many slaves. Like Moses, she led her people to freedom. Tubman's work was very dangerous, but she never lost a single person.

Anthony Burns

Not every slave who escaped stayed free. Anthony Burns worked as a slave in a shipyard in Virginia. He made friends with the sailors. One day a sailor helped him escape by ship to Boston. When Burns's master found out where Burns lived, the master traveled to Boston to get him back. The master captured Burns one night while he walked home from work.

Anthony Burns

Many people in Boston supported Burns. They wanted him to be free. A mob even tried to free him but failed. The president sent soldiers to guard Burns. When the case went to court, the judge ruled that Burns must return with his master. The master treated Burns harshly for running away. Later some free black Americans raised enough money to buy Burns's freedom.

The Boston Slave Riot, art by John B. Rolic

Two Views

Stories like Burns's made people in the free states angry. They wanted to keep slavery out of their states. Many of them thought that slavery was wrong. But the Compromise of 1850 said runaway slaves found in free states had to be returned. Slave owners could claim slaves as property.

These stories made people in the slave states angry as well. Slave owners believed slaves were their property. The slave owner thought a slave stole himself when he ran away. If people tried to stop a slave owner from getting his slave back, the slave owner thought they were stealing from him.

The problem of runaway slaves divided the country. This problem raised an important question. Should people be allowed to own other people as property?

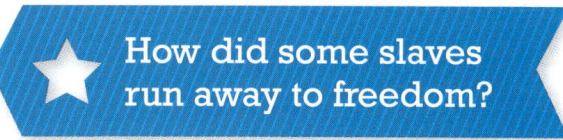
How did some slaves run away to freedom?

Voting for Slavery: Right or Wrong?

Stephen Douglas's Plan

As Americans moved west, they brought the problems of slavery with them. Many people wanted to build a railroad so they could move to different places faster. They wanted to connect California to the eastern states. Senator Stephen Douglas thought the tracks should run west of his home state, Illinois. But he needed permission from the national government to build this railroad. He needed support from as many states as possible, including both free and slave states.

Douglas needed to give the slave states something they wanted. Then they would help him get what he wanted. The Missouri Compromise did not allow slaves in some territories. Douglas's plan was to let people in all US territories vote to be free or slave once they became states.

Douglas thought voting made sense. It gave people the choice of slavery. Many people in the North did not agree. They did not want more slavery. Slavery continued to divide America.

Right and Wrong

Abraham Lincoln was a politician from Illinois who ran against Douglas. He did not like people voting to have or not have slaves. He thought that owning people was wrong. The first Congress of America did not allow slavery in the territories. Lincoln thought the founders had made a wise decision.

Slave owners did not agree with Lincoln. They said that people from free states took their animals to any state. So slave owners should be able to take their slaves to any state. But Lincoln said that animals and people were different. People should be treated better than animals.

Slave owners argued that their freedom to own slaves was being taken away. But Lincoln said doing right was more important than having the freedom to own slaves. Owning people was wrong. It was wrong to give people the choice to own people.

American slave auction

Kansas

People in Kansas wanted to make a choice on slavery. They thought they should vote to be a free or slave state. People who liked or hated slavery rushed to Kansas. They wanted to pick what Kansas would be.

Hand-colored woodcut of Bleeding Kansas, 1850s

When Kansas had an election to decide on its new leaders, many people broke the law. Some people from Missouri who supported slavery came and voted in Kansas. This was against the law. They picked leaders who wanted slavery. People against slavery held their own election. They made their own government for Kansas.

The two sides tried to harm each other. Some people who wanted slavery burned homes and businesses. No one was hurt. One person who wanted to get even was John Brown. He hated slavery. Brown killed five people who supported slavery in Kansas. People called the area "Bleeding Kansas" as fighting spread. The fighting in Kansas further divided the slave states and the free states.

Dred Scott

What: slave
When: 1795–1858
Where: Virginia

Born into slavery, Dred Scott sued for his freedom. The Supreme Court ruled that Scott remain a slave. Eventually, Scott's owners gave him his freedom. His headstone reads: "In memory of a simple man who wanted to be free." Dred Scott's efforts show the great value of freedom.

Dred Scott

Dred Scott's story also divided the nation. Scott was a slave who had lived with his owner in a free state. Scott said he should be free since he had lived in a free state. This case went to court. Several courts did not agree on a decision in Scott's case. Finally, the Supreme Court made a decision.

The Supreme Court said that no black person could be a citizen of the United States. The court also said that no state or territory could make slavery illegal. The Constitution did not allow the national government to take away people's property. Since slaves were thought of as property, slavery was legal. People who did not like slavery were angry. The Supreme Court decision further divided the people.

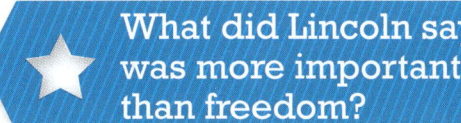

What did Lincoln say was more important than freedom?

Points of View

Views in the North and the South

Most Americans had strong views on slavery even before the Dred Scott case. Most people in the South said that slavery was necessary to their way of life. They said that owning slaves made life better for both slaves and free people.

The two parts of the United States had very different ways of life. People in each part thought their way of life was better. The free states in the North had more factories. The slave states in the South had more farms. Some slave states thought the free states were too interested in making money. The southerners felt that the northerners were selfish. And some northerners felt that the southerners were wrong to treat other human beings as property.

People in the South believed they had better values than people in the North. Southerners thought duty, honor, and courage were more important than making money. Southerners also thought life for the slaves was better than life for factory workers in the North. People in the South said they thought of their slaves as part of their families. Southerners claimed to treat slaves well.

But northerners said that southern culture could not be good. It did not give workers their freedom. Northerners said northern workers were free to find better jobs. But slaves could not leave one master for a better one. These slaves could not have freedom.

Many people in the South believed the Bible allowed people to own slaves. These southerners believed the Bible taught that slaves should obey their masters.

Black American Views

Black Americans did not agree with most southerners. Many black Americans who wrote about slavery believed the Bible and respected its teachings. They believed the Bible taught it was unkind to make people slaves. The writers pointed out Matthew 7:12, which says "Whatsoever ye would that men should do to you, do ye even so to them." This verse is called the Golden Rule. Black writers asked these questions: Would slave owners want to be slaves? If not, then how could slave owners say it was right to make slaves of others?

Few slave owners allowed slaves to learn to read. These slaves could not read the Bible for themselves. Reading the Bible for themselves would have helped them worship and grow in Christ.

Slave housing

Daniel Coker

What: minister
When: 1780–1846
Where: Maryland

Daniel Coker was a minister in the African Methodist Episcopal Church in America. He said the Bible did not permit kidnapping Africans for slavery. The Bible also did not allow the slaves' children to be kept as slaves.

Black Americans said that slavery in Bible times was different from slavery in the South. Slaves in the United States were captured people from Africa. The Bible forbids stealing people. In the Bible the punishment for stealing a person was death. In Israel a person could become a slave to pay money he owed. The Bible also says to free slaves after six years of service. Then masters were to provide everything those freed slaves needed to begin a new life. In the Bible runaway slaves were not to be returned to their masters. Slaves were set free if they were harmed.

Slave owners in the South did not follow Bible teachings about slaves. Many American slaves had been stolen from their homes in Africa. Few owners freed their slaves. Many slaves were harmed.

 What is Matthew 7:12 called?

Life as a Slave

Slave Homes and Jobs

Life as a slave was not the same in all places. Some slaves worked alongside their owners. A slave often lived in the *loft* of the owner's cabin. Other slaves worked on large plantations. They worked in groups under a boss. Some slaves worked from morning to night in the fields. Others were given a list of jobs to do. They could work in their own gardens when their list was finished.

Slaves did many kinds of jobs. Some worked in their owners' house as cooks or servants. Some made sure the buildings, fences, and farm tools were kept in good shape. Some took care of the animals. Many slaves worked in the fields. Often these were cotton fields. In some parts of the South, slaves worked in rice or sugarcane plantations.

a slave's loft

Treatment of Enslaved People

Slave owners wanted to show that slavery was good. Some owners tried to treat slaves well. But slavery is wrong. So even those who tried to do their best did not treat slaves right.

Often slave owners did not give slaves the respect they deserved. Some slaves were not allowed to name their children. Instead, slave owners named them. Some slave owners decided which slaves would marry each other. Some owners chose the slaves' pastors. Few owners allowed slaves to learn to read. These things often offended enslaved people.

Sometimes slave owners had to make hard choices. For example, some slave owners said they did not like to separate slave families. But when owners needed money, slave families were sold away from each other. Owners sold children away from their parents. These children had to grow up at another plantation. If an owner chose to, he could even separate a husband and wife.

Owners made their slaves work hard and obey. If a slave displeased a master, the slave would often receive a cruel and painful punishment. Some masters forced slaves to watch as friends or family suffered. Most slaves could not ask courts for help.

Importance of Enslaved People

Many people believed a person's skin color made him important or unimportant. Thinking this way led to the sinful treatment of the slaves. Many people believed that people with black skin were only fit to be slaves. The Bible does not teach this idea. God says that He "made of one blood all nations of men" (Acts 17:26). God made all people in His image. Every person has the same rights because he is made in God's image.

Anti-slavery drawing

Slaves understood their true value as human beings. Some slaves had strong family ties. Some slaves had their own churches. They loved Bible accounts where the children of Israel were freed. Slaves made up songs of these Bible accounts. Slaves working on larger plantations had more friends to sing and tell stories with. They looked for small ways to find good in life.

Five generations of a Beaufort, SC, slave family

 What does the Bible teach about how all people should be treated?

Singing Spirituals

Spirituals are religious folk songs that slaves made up to help them bear their work and sorrow. Spirituals tell about the slaves' faith in God to protect and deliver them.

Northern Views on Slavery

Free States' View

Many free states thought that the slave states wanted to control the whole nation. These people thought it was not fair that slaves counted as part of the population. Free states worried that slavery might spread into the territories. Slave states would then run the country.

White people in the North did not like slavery. But this did not mean they liked black people. Even in the North many white people thought they were better than black people. These Americans believed that black people should not be treated the same as white people. Many thought skin color made people unequal. Many did not want black people to have the right to vote.

Abraham Lincoln's View

Abraham Lincoln believed that black people should have the same rights given in the Declaration of Independence. He believed all people had the rights of life, liberty, and the pursuit of happiness. But he said that it was up to the states to decide if black people could vote. Lincoln knew most people would not want black people to have the right to vote.

Abraham Lincoln

Abolitionists' View

Some people thought slavery should end immediately. They were known as **abolitionists**. The word *abolish* means to end. Abolitionists wanted to end slavery in the United States. They started newspapers, held meetings, and wrote books. They wanted to win people to their side. John Brown was an abolitionist. He even tried to to stop slavery by fighting.

Most people thought that the abolitionists were going too far. Even those who wanted slavery to end thought this. They thought the abolitionists would break apart the country. In the end, everybody would suffer.

Slavery Divides America

Some people wanted to end slavery so it would not spread to the territories. These people wanted to see the slaves freed one day. But they also did not want to see the country be divided. They hoped slavery would die off.

But attacks on slavery grew stronger, and Americans began to lose their unity. People in the South defended slavery as good and necessary. People in the North feared that slave owners were gaining too much power. The Americans no longer wanted to compromise.

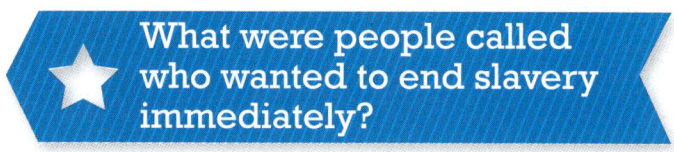

What were people called who wanted to end slavery immediately?

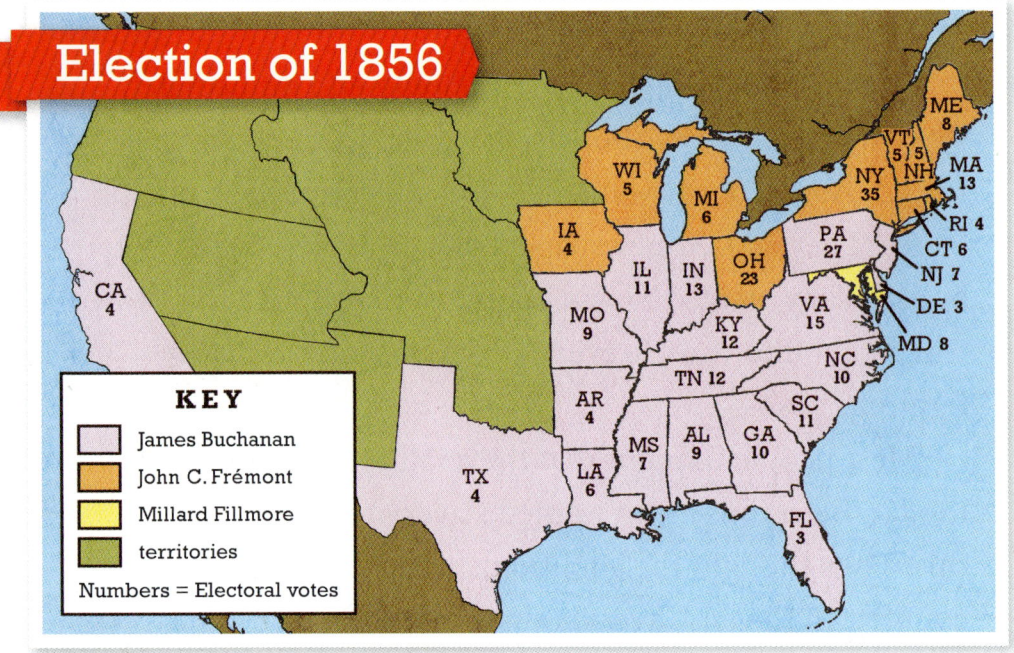

Election of 1856

The argument over slavery had an effect on political parties. The Whigs did not agree with each other on slavery. They divided in the election of 1856. Most Whigs from the North were against slavery. They voted to start a new party. It was called the **Republican Party**. Most Whigs in the South owned slaves. These Whigs voted to start a party called the American Party.

The Democrats stuck together. They chose James Buchanan to run for president. He was from the North but also supported the South. Buchanan won the election with votes from both the North and the South. However, he had a hard time while president. Arguments over slavery continued. He did not deal with them well.

Abraham Lincoln

Abraham Lincoln was born in a log cabin in Kentucky in 1809. His family was very poor, and his parents could not read or write. Abraham and his sister studied at a one-room schoolhouse for a few years. He had his first lessons in numbers, reading, and writing.

Abraham worked hard helping his father on the farm. Often Abraham could not go to school. But he borrowed books and newspapers. He learned all he could on his own.

Log cabin representing the birthplace of Abraham Lincoln

Lincoln grew up to be a tall, thin man. He was six feet and four inches, towering over nearly everyone. He worked at a store in Illinois. Lincoln liked speaking and politics. He became a lawmaker for the state government of Illinois. He also studied law on his own. He passed his law exams and became a lawyer. Lincoln married a wealthy young woman named Mary Todd. They had four sons.

Lincoln joined the US House of Representatives. In 1858 he ran against Stephen Douglas to be part of the Senate. Lincoln lost. But people knew Lincoln by now. They had heard him speak in public. This made him famous and helped him get elected as president in 1860.

Election of 1860

In the election of 1860, the Democrats were divided. They voted for different people to run for president. Democrats in the North voted for Stephen Douglas. He believed that territories should have the right to vote for slavery or against slavery. Democrats in the South voted for a man who wanted to allow slavery in all the territories.

Most people in the North liked the Republican Party. Its members were called Republicans. They wanted to protect manufacturing in the North. This party was also against slavery in the new territories. However, the Republicans promised not to end slavery in the slave states. The Republicans picked Abraham Lincoln to run for president.

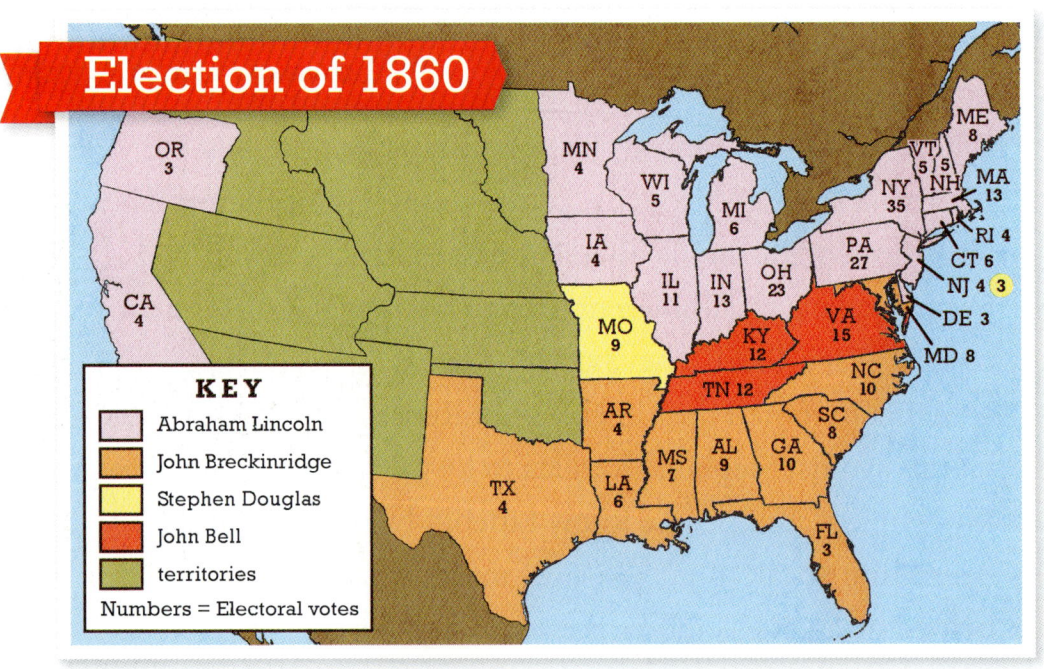

Abraham Lincoln won enough votes and became president. None of the votes had come from the South. They had all come from the North. This greatly worried people in the South. A president had never before been elected by only one part of the country. The South feared that Lincoln would only care about the people who elected him. Southerners feared he would harm the South.

Slave owners were afraid of losing their slaves. Lincoln tried to calm the slave owners. He said that he would not end slavery in the slave states. But he said he would not allow slavery in the territories. People in the South worried that the territories would turn into free states. They worried that slave states would lose their power in Congress. They did not trust Lincoln.

Lincoln's first inauguration, 1861

America Divides

The southern states were unhappy with the election. They did not trust the new president to protect their slaves. Five states met to talk about separating from the United States. They wanted to leave or **secede** from the United States. In December 1860, South Carolina seceded from the United States. Six other states followed.

South Carolina said it left the United States because some free states in the North did not obey the Constitution. The Constitution said that runaway slaves should be returned. It also said that slaves were property. But some northern states said that slaves could be free when they went into some free states. South Carolina said the Constitution did not allow this. South Carolina also said that states should not allow black people to be US citizens or to vote. South Carolina said that it had the right to secede because some free states did not obey the Constitution. It was now up to the new president to decide how to deal with the split nation. Abraham Lincoln faced big decisions.

What finally divided the American nation?

10 The Civil War

Focus

The Civil War divided the nation between the North and the South.

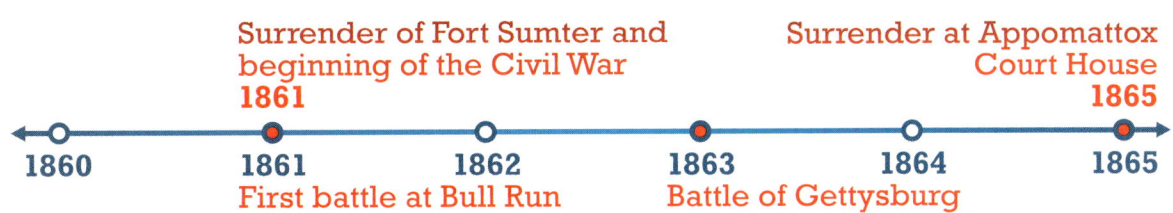

War Begins

Southern States Secede

Abraham Lincoln was president. By now seven states in the South had decided to secede from the United States. To secede means to leave. These states joined to form a confederation. A confederation is a group that pledges, or promises, to work together.

The seven southern states called themselves the **Confederate States of America**. They chose Jefferson Davis as their president. They also chose Richmond, Virginia, as their capital. They wanted to have their own country.

Lincoln asked the southern states to stay in the United States. He promised to let them keep their slaves. But he also said that they had no right to secede. The states would not listen.

Fort Sumter

The United States owned a fort in Charleston, South Carolina. The commander of the fort sent Lincoln a message. The fort needed more food. Lincoln had a hard choice. South Carolina was one of the seven states that had seceded. If he sent a ship with food to the fort, South Carolina's soldiers might shoot the ship. If he did not send the ship, soldiers at the fort would starve.

Lincoln thought about taking the US soldiers out of the fort. Instead, he sent the South Carolina governor a message. Lincoln said that that he would send only food to Fort Sumter. He promised he would not send men or weapons.

Surrender

Citizens of the Confederate States were called Confederates. The Confederates did not want a US army in the South. The Confederate president Jefferson Davis got Lincoln's message to South Carolina. Davis said that Fort Sumter must surrender to the Confederates.

But the fort did not surrender. On April 12, 1861, the Confederate army shot at it with cannons. The US soldiers in the fort fought back until they used all their ammunition. *Ammunition* is anything that can be fired from a weapon and cause harm. In the end the US soldiers surrendered. The **Civil War** had begun.

Bombardment of Fort Sumter, Charleston Harbor, 1861

Lincoln asked states to send militias to fight for the United States. A **militia** is a group of citizens who are trained to defend their country. Soon the northern states sent more soldiers than needed. These states wanted the United States to stay together.

More States Secede

The southern states that had not seceded did not know what to do. They wanted to stay in the United States. But they did not want to fight against the southern states that had seceded.

Seceding States

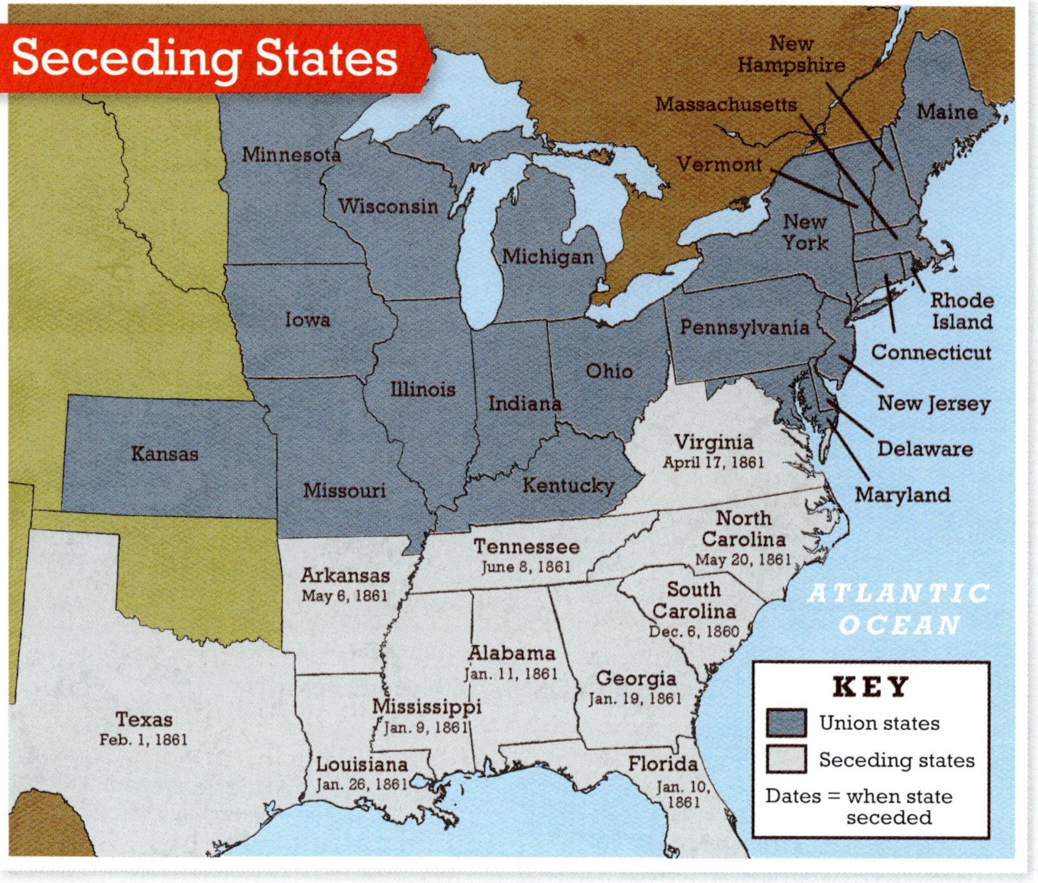

New Hampshire
Massachusetts
Maine
Vermont
Minnesota
Wisconsin
Michigan
New York
Rhode Island
Iowa
Pennsylvania
Connecticut
Illinois
Ohio
Indiana
New Jersey
Kansas
Virginia
April 17, 1861
Delaware
Missouri
Kentucky
Maryland
North Carolina
May 20, 1861
Tennessee
June 8, 1861
Arkansas
May 6, 1861
South Carolina
Dec. 6, 1860
ATLANTIC OCEAN
Alabama
Jan. 11, 1861
Georgia
Jan. 19, 1861
Mississippi
Jan. 9, 1861
Texas
Feb. 1, 1861
Louisiana
Jan. 26, 1861
Florida
Jan. 10, 1861
KEY
Union states
Seceding states
Dates = when state seceded

When Lincoln asked the states for soldiers, each state had to choose which side to fight for—the United States or the Confederate States. Four more southern states decided to join the Confederate States. Four slave states chose to stay part of the United States.

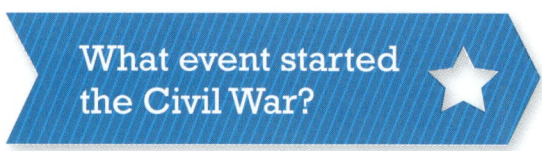

What event started the Civil War?

Both Sides Make Plans

The North

All of the North and some of the South were still part of the United States. At this time the United States was sometimes called the North or the **Union**. All of the Confederate States were from the South. They were sometimes called the South or the **Confederacy**.

Neither the North nor the South was ready for war. The US Army was small. Its troops were far away, west of the Mississippi River. The Confederate states were still forming their government in Richmond, Virginia. But both sides still had advantages over the other side.

The North had more men to fight in its army. The North also had more factories. They could make uniforms, shoes, guns, cannons, and other things that were useful for war. There were also more railroads in the North. Railroads helped move men and equipment quickly.

The North had some disadvantages. The US Army would have to go to the South to fight. The Union soldiers would be far from home. They would need to take food and supplies with them.

The South

The Southern states had their own advantages. The southerners would be fighting on their own land. When an army goes far away to attack, it needs more men and supplies. An army that is defending close to home needs fewer men and supplies.

The South also had good soldiers. Before the Civil War, more southern men than northern men had served in the US Army. When the Civil War began, most of these men returned home to the South to fight for the Confederacy. The South had many good generals. Thomas J. "Stonewall" Jackson, James Longstreet, and J. E. B. Stuart were just a few of these skilled men. The Confederates thought that the North would soon get tired of war and give up.

Compare Sides in the Civil War		
	United States of America	Confederate States of America
Location	Mostly northern states	Most southern states
President	Abraham Lincoln	Jefferson Davis
Capital	Washington, DC	Richmond, Virginia
Slave or Free	Free states, some slave states	Most slave states
Nicknames	Union, USA, North	Confederacy, CSA, South
Soldiers	Greater number	Better trained
Advantages	More factories to produce supplies and more railroads to transport supplies	Fighting close to home, little need to travel far

Robert E. Lee

The South's best general, **Robert E. Lee**, had a hard choice. He was asked to lead the northern armies. Lee turned this offer down.

But Lee also did not want to fight against the United States. He thought it was a bad idea to secede from the nation. Lee said that if he could free all the slaves in the South to stop a war, he would. But he also thought that a Union kept together by force was not worth much.

Robert E. Lee

Lee hoped that his state, Virginia, would stay in the Union. When it seceded, Lee said he could not fight against his home state. Instead, he felt it was his duty to defend it. Lee served in the southern army for the whole war.

Winfield Scott

General Winfield Scott led the US Army. He was older than most other officers and was a smart general. To win the war he planned to blockade the South. The US Navy would stop ships from going in or out of any southern port. Scott knew that the South made its money by selling cotton to other countries. The South also bought imports from them. A blockade would hurt the South.

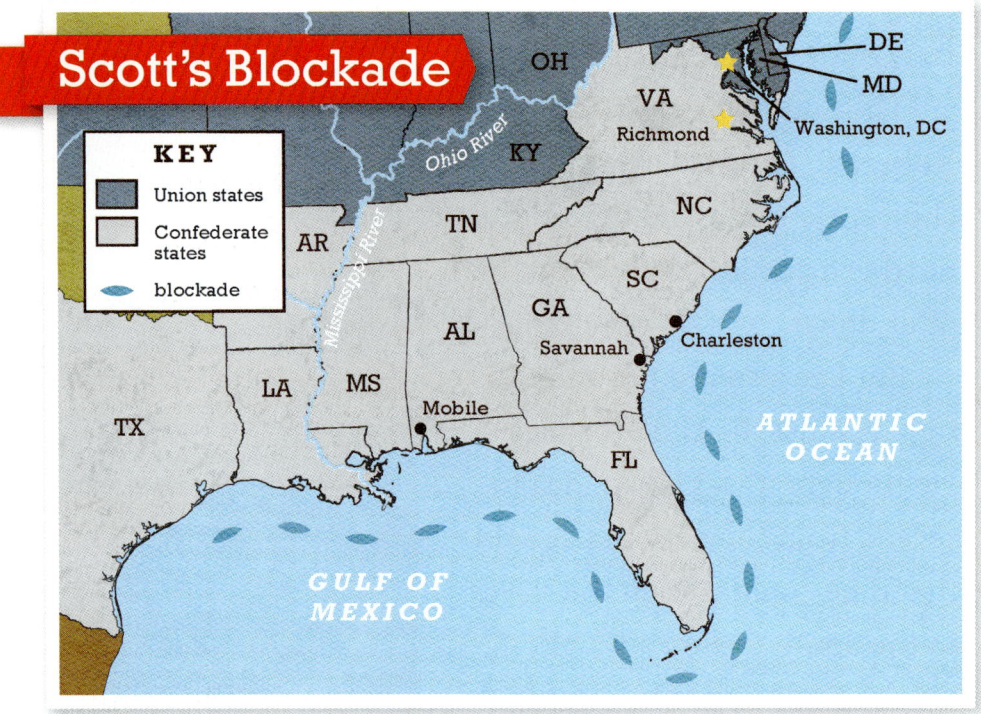

General Scott also planned to take control of the Mississippi River. He would cut off Texas, Louisiana, and Arkansas from the rest of the South. Scott thought that the Union would take several years to defeat the Confederacy.

Many in the North did not like Scott's plan. They thought it would take much too long. They thought the war could end more quickly. The Confederacy's capital was in Richmond, Virginia. People thought the US Army should just march straight to Richmond and defeat the Confederacy. But both General Scott and General Lee knew the war would last many years.

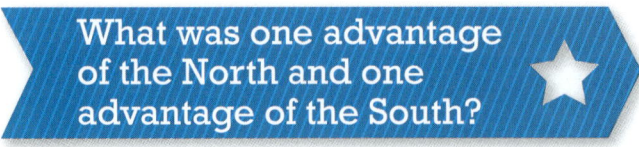

What was one advantage of the North and one advantage of the South?

Early Battles
Battle of Bull Run

By July of 1861, President Lincoln thought it was time to fight. The Union army marched toward Richmond, Virginia. The Confederate army waited for them at the town of Manassas, Virginia, near a stream called Bull Run.

Some people traveled down from Washington, DC, to watch the battle. They thought the Union army would beat the Confederate army. At first the Union forces did well. They attacked where the Confederates did not expect and surprised them.

But the Confederates held their ground. One southern general told his men to stand firm. He pointed to General Thomas Jackson and shouted, "There is Jackson standing like a stone wall!" From then on people called him "**Stonewall**" Jackson.

Thomas "Stonewall" Jackson

It seemed like the Union forces would win. But then trains came and brought another Confederate army. It came to join the fight. The Union army could not hold the Confederate army back. Soon the Union army retreated to Washington. The South won the **Battle of Bull Run**.

The North realized that fighting the South would not be easy. The Union would need to prepare better.

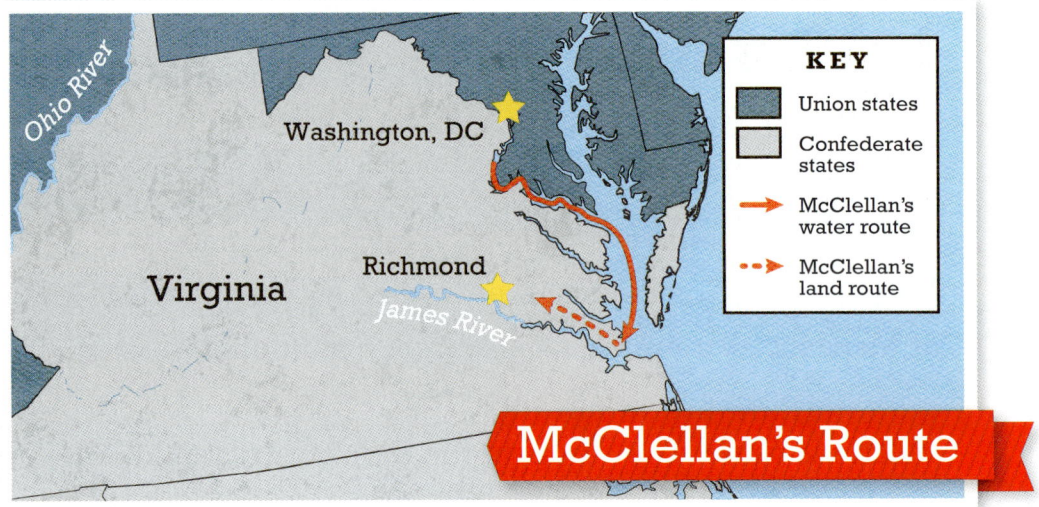

To Richmond from the Sea

After the Union lost the Battle of Bull Run, Lincoln found a new general to lead the US Army. General **George B. McClellan** knew how to run an army. He taught new volunteers to be good soldiers. He made sure the men had good uniforms and guns. Over and over again he trained the men to march and fight. But McClellan was better at planning than fighting.

McClellan came up with a plan. The Union army would sail to the Virginia coast. They could then march west to Richmond. The Confederate army would not expect the Union army to come from the east. At first McClellan's plan seemed to work. But he moved too slowly. The Confederate army had time to move their troops and block the way to Richmond. McClellan was afraid that the Confederates had more men than they really did. After several battles, McClellan retreated.

Battles in the West

The Union forces had more success fighting in the West. Union general **Ulysses S. Grant** attacked two Confederate forts. The forts were built along rivers.

Grant ordered his gunboats to fire at the forts. At the same time, his army attacked the forts by land. Grant successfully captured both forts and thousands of Confederate soldiers.

The Union army also wanted to capture a city in Mississippi called Corinth. This was where the Confederacy's main railroads in the West met. The South used these railroads to move many troops and goods. The Union wanted to stop them.

Ulysses S. Grant

The Confederate generals grew worried. They hurried to attack Grant before he got to the city. At the **Battle of Shiloh**, the Confederate army surprised Grant. They fought hard. Thousands of men died. But the Union army won in the end. Americans on both sides began to realize that this would be a long and costly war.

Battle of Antietam

Union forces in the East continued to have problems. Lincoln tried many generals. But no one could beat General Lee or capture the Confederate capital. Union armies still kept fighting in Virginia.

After General Lee won a second battle at Bull Run, he moved the war to the North. First, Lee needed guns and ammunition. He sent Stonewall Jackson to capture Union goods. Then Lee made plans to defeat the Union army. But someone in the Confederate army lost a copy of the plans. A Union soldier found them.

Once General McClellan had the plans, he could beat Lee's armies. The North's army attacked at Antietam in Maryland. The Battle of Antietam was one of the most terrible battles of the war. Both sides lost many men. Over twenty thousand soldiers were killed or wounded in one day. McClellan could have defeated Lee at this battle. But McClellan was still too cautious. He let Lee escape south.

Still, because the Confederate army withdrew, the North thought of the Battle of Antietam as a victory.

Battle of Fredericksburg

After the Battle of Antietam, Lincoln chose a new general named Ambrose Burnside. General Burnside marched south to surprise General Lee. Burnside and his men reached a town called Fredericksburg. They needed to cross a river there. They built bridges to cross it, but this took a long time.

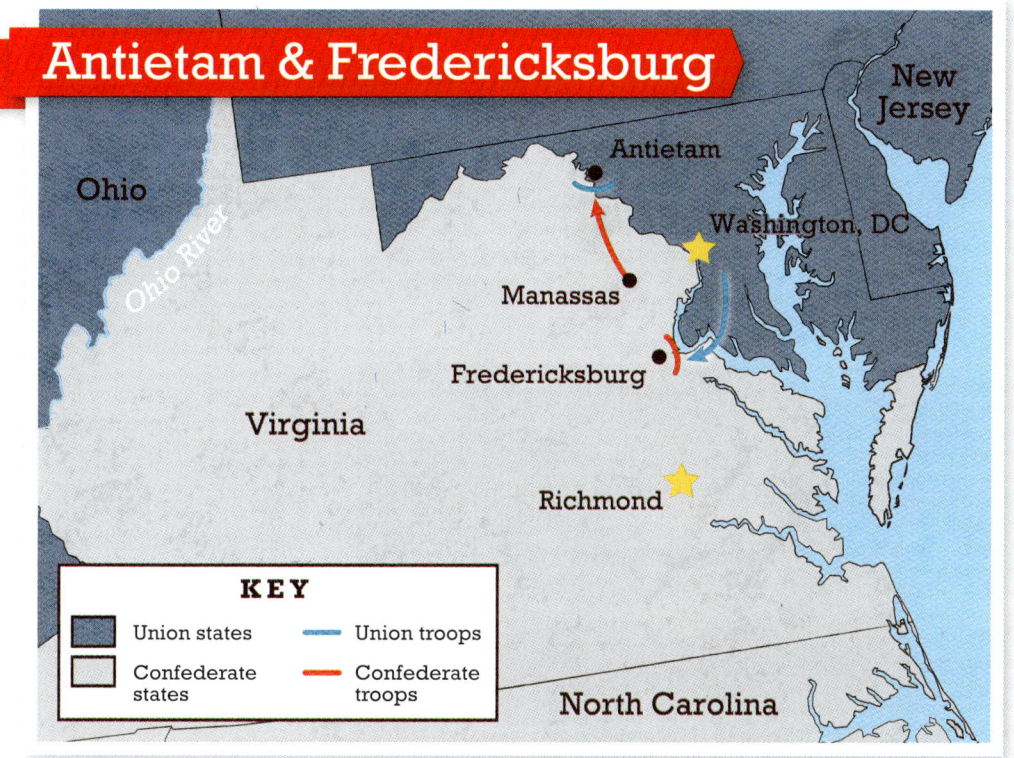

Lee found out where Burnside was. Lee had time to move his men to a good location. There they would be strong and ready for Burnside's army. When Burnside and his men crossed the river, Lee's army was ready to defend itself. Burnside attacked but could not defeat Lee's army.

In these early battles of the Civil War, there was much fighting. But the Union could not succeed in capturing Richmond, the Confederate capital. And the Confederates did not succeed in their invasion of the North.

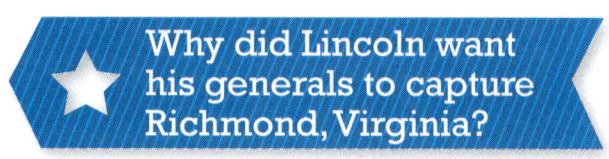
Why did Lincoln want his generals to capture Richmond, Virginia?

The Emancipation Proclamation

Lincoln's Announcement

Lincoln hated slavery. For a long time he wished that the United States did not allow slavery. But he knew that the Constitution gave permission for slavery. It did not let the president free all the slaves.

The first reading of the Emancipation Proclamation before the cabinet

Lincoln could not free slaves in states that were loyal to the Union. But he had the power to declare some slaves free in states that had seceded from the Union.

The Union's victory at the Battle of Antietam made people trust Lincoln more. At this time, he signed a document called the **Emancipation Proclamation**. A **proclamation** is an official public announcement. To emancipate means to set free. The Emancipation Proclamation set slaves free in territories that had rebelled against the Union. This meant that slaves in the Confederate States would be free.

Some Enslaved People Emancipated

Before the Civil War, Lincoln thought that freeing slaves would take a long time. He thought that slave owners would need to be paid if they gave up slaves. And he knew that people in the states would have to vote to free the slaves.

As the war went on, it seemed like the Union would win. Lincoln realized that once the Union won the war, the country could not have both free and slave states. A final decision had to be made about slavery.

Many enslaved people in the South had already fled from their owners to safety with the Union army. Because of the Emancipation Proclamation, slave owners could not take these people back after the Civil War. Slaves in the Confederate States would also remain free after the war.

Emancipation Proclamation document, 1863

Fresh Union Regiments

After the Emancipation Proclamation, some black Americans joined the Union Army. They wanted to fight for the freedom of all black Americans.

Enslaved black Americans who were now free formed black *regiments*, or groups of soldiers. These men gained much respect. Their new regiments provided fresh, courageous soldiers. These soldiers fought well and became loyal citizens.

Soldiers from a black regiment, Dutch Gap, Virginia, 1864

The Thirteenth Amendment

Some people did not like the Emancipation Proclamation. They said it claimed to free slaves in areas where Lincoln had no power. In the South many slave owners still kept slaves working. The Confederates did not even think of Lincoln as their president.

Celebration of the Thirteenth Amendment being passed, 1862

But the Emancipation Proclamation changed the country. The proclamation showed that slavery would end. After the Civil War, the United States would not be divided between free states and slave states. All the states would be free.

President Lincoln urged Congress to pass a new amendment to the Constitution. He wanted to end slavery in all the states. This law passed after the war ended. The law is the **Thirteenth Amendment** to the Constitution.

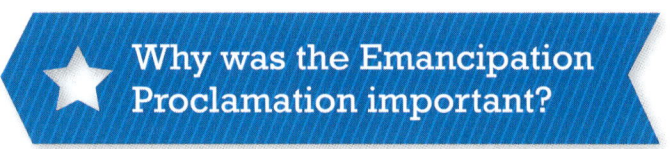

Why was the Emancipation Proclamation important?

The War at Sea

Blockade Runners

Americans fought the Civil War on sea as well as on land. The US Navy put a blockade on the southern ports. Union ships stopped ships loaded with cotton from leaving the ports. Since the South could not sell its cotton, southerners had little money to buy the things they needed. The Confederacy had few factories to make guns and war supplies. Stopping war supplies from being shipped hurt the South.

But putting a blockade on the southern ports was a difficult task. The southern coast stretched for hundreds of miles. Daring and fast *blockade runners* often slipped past the US Navy ships. These small, light boats brought war supplies and food to the South. But over time the blockade tightened. The US Navy built more ships and gained control of some southern ports.

Battle between the *Monitor*, a US ship, and the *Virginia*, a Confederate ship

Ironclad Ships

When the war started, the Confederates had only a few small ships. The South had no way to build more ships. But a man in charge of the Confederate navy had an idea. There was one ship that the US Navy had left behind in the South. The Confederate navy could turn this ship into an **ironclad ship**. The whole ship above the water would be covered in iron. This was a new type of ship. Workers mounted cannons onto the ship. The South called the ship the CSS *Virginia*.

The *Virginia* traveled out to the coast to meet the blockade of wooden US Navy ships. They fired at the new ship. But the cannonballs bounced off the *Virginia*'s iron sides. The *Virginia* sank one Union ship and battered another until that ship surrendered.

The next day the *Virginia* traveled out again. But it met a surprise. The US Navy had made its own ironclad ship. For three hours, the two ships fought, but neither could sink the other. The cannonballs just bounced off both ships. The Union kept its blockade.

New Inventions Used in the War

Better Guns

During the Civil War, both sides used new inventions. Most soldiers used guns called muskets. But muskets were slow to use. They had to be loaded from the front and could fire only one shot at a time.

Inventors made better guns. One was called the breech-loading rifle. It could be loaded from the back. Another gun was what soldiers called a repeating rifle. It could fire seven times before it had to be reloaded. Soldiers on horseback liked this rifle because it was easier to use while riding.

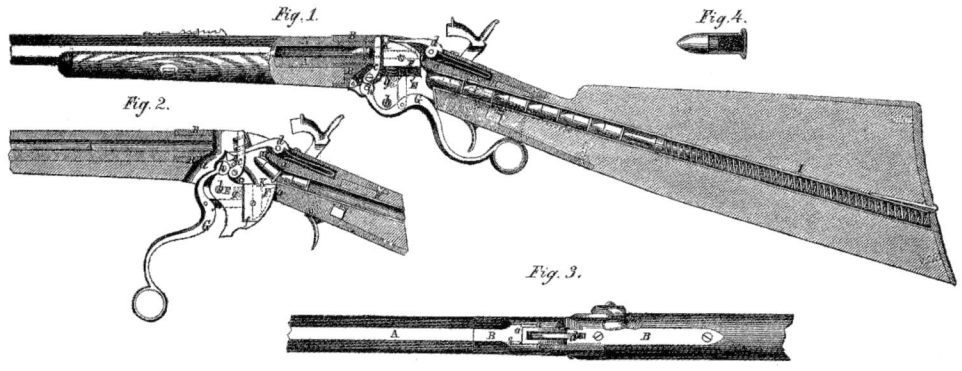

Spencer repeating rifle, one of the guns used in the Civil War

More Railroads

Railroads had new uses during the war. Before railroads, soldiers had to march from one battle location to another. Now generals could quickly move their troops on trains. Railroads also brought supplies to the soldiers.

The Telegraph

The telegraph was also useful during the war. Union general Grant used the telegraph in a special way. He had his troops lay telegraph lines as they moved forward. This way he could let his commanding general know what he was doing. Later when Grant became the main general, he told those who served under him to lay telegraph lines too.

What were some inventions used during the Civil War?

Deciphering and Writing Morse Code

Army officers were able to send messages by telegraph in Morse code. Communication by telegraph was faster and more reliable than sending messages by a person riding a horse.

Clara Barton

Clara Barton worked hard at every job she had. After success in teaching and office work, Barton became a nurse. During the Civil War, she risked her life to help the wounded. After the war, Barton set up the American Red Cross. Her work still continues to help people today.

Victories for the North
Gettysburg, Pennsylvania

Many people wondered if anyone could beat Confederate general Robert E. Lee. But Lee knew the war needed to end soon for the Confederate States to stay independent. The US Navy blockade hurt them. The South did not have enough food. Lee's army needed supplies too. Lee marched his army into the North to Pennsylvania for supplies.

In Pennsylvania, Lee's army fought the Union army in a small town called Gettysburg. Lee tried to push back the Union army. Many men on both sides died. Lee could not push out the Union forces. After three days of battle, Lee had lost too many men. He retreated back to Virginia. The **Battle of Gettysburg** ended southern hopes of defeating the Union.

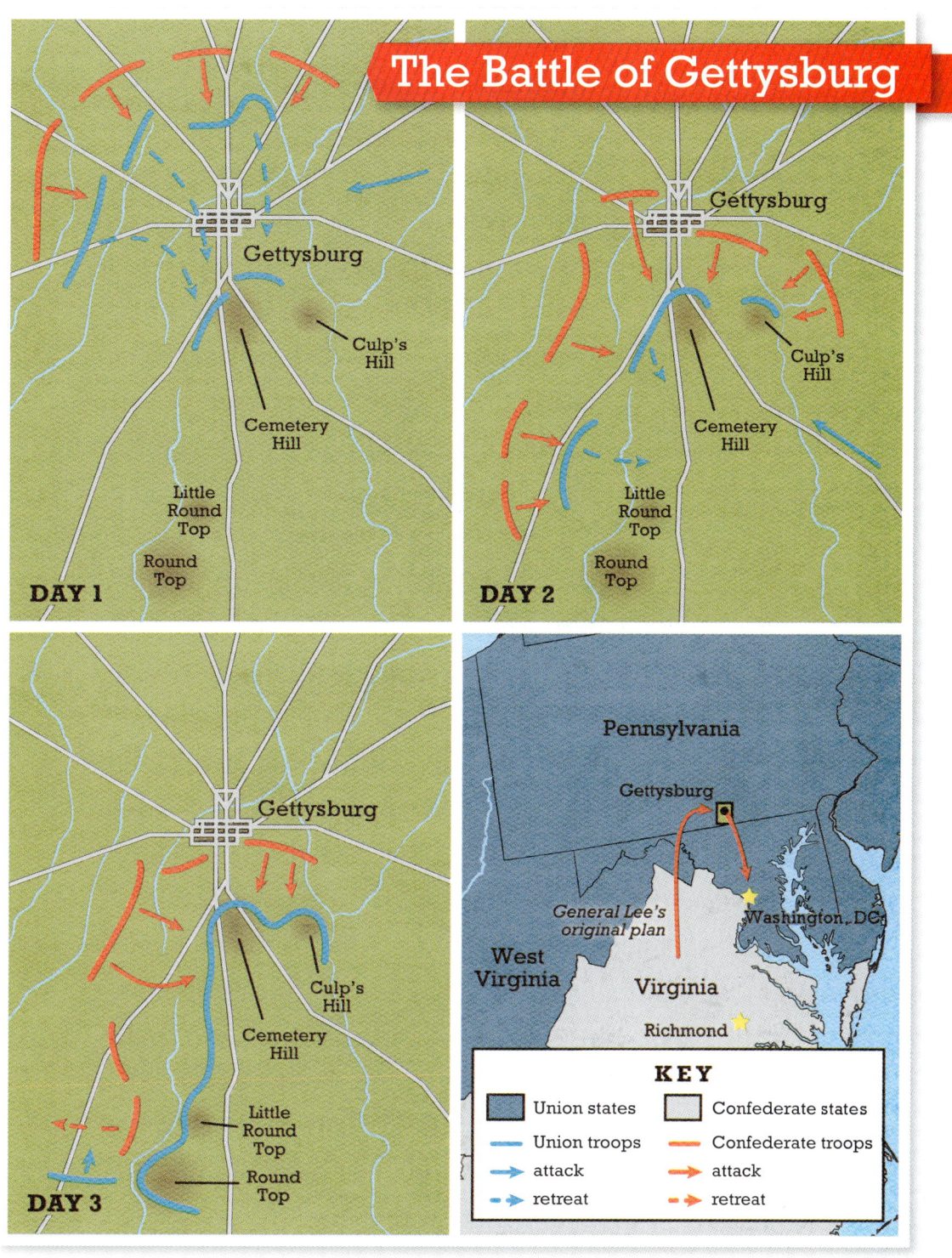

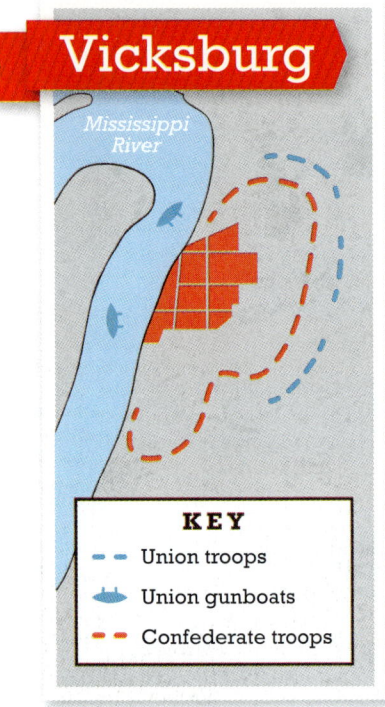

Vicksburg, Mississippi

Another important victory for the Union was the capture of the city of Vicksburg, Mississippi. Vicksburg sat on the banks of the Mississippi River. It was the last city on the Mississippi River that was under Confederate control. Union forces controlled the river north and south of Vicksburg. Union general Grant put gunboats on the river near the city. Then he put his army on the other side of the city. Vicksburg was trapped. Grant waited until the city had no food left, and Vicksburg surrendered.

After the battle at Vicksburg, President Lincoln realized that he had found the right general to lead all the Union forces. Grant knew when to fight and when to wait. Lincoln put him in charge of all the Union armies. Grant stayed with one army and commanded it in person. He had other generals lead the other armies. But they all were under General Grant's command. Grant's army led the march to capture the Confederate capital of Richmond, Virginia.

In Virginia, Grant attacked Lee's army again and again. Lee used all of his skill to block Grant. But it was not enough. Grant knew that he could weaken Lee's army. Lee could not afford to lose men. Grant lost many soldiers too. People thought too many men were dying.

Sherman's March

One of the Union generals under Grant was William Sherman. He fought in the South. He captured the city of Atlanta, Georgia. Then his army marched toward the seacoast. The army took food from families in Georgia. But then the soldiers did more. They killed animals that they did not need for food. They destroyed railroads and buildings and food growing in the fields. Sherman marched east to the sea and then north. He left ruin wherever he went.

Sherman's army destroying railroad tracks

Christians sometimes talk about right ways and wrong ways to fight wars. Many Christians believe that when armies fight, they may harm only people fighting in the other army. Sherman did not agree. He wanted to end the war quickly. Sherman showed little mercy to those not fighting. He destroyed nearly everything in his path.

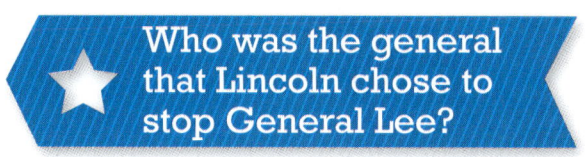
Who was the general that Lincoln chose to stop General Lee?

Lee's surrender at Appomattox Court House

Surrender at Last

By the spring of 1865, the Confederacy was failing. Grant was near the Confederate capital, Richmond, and Lee could no longer hold him off. Lee tried to slip away from Richmond to help fight General Sherman in North Carolina. But Grant blocked Lee every time he tried to get away. Finally, Lee agreed to surrender to Grant. They met at a town called **Appomattox Court House** in Virginia.

President Lincoln told Grant to be kind during the surrender. He said Grant should let the men keep their horses and guns. They would need the horses to plow their fields. They could use the guns to shoot crows that might eat the seeds they planted. President Lincoln wanted peace.

The Struggle for Peace

Lincoln knew it was important to bring about peace as the war came to an end. The North and the South needed to live together again as one nation. They needed to work as one people.

In 1864 Americans elected Lincoln to a second term as president. As he started the new term, Lincoln gave a speech. He encouraged the country to unite and live in peace. He warned the northerners not to seek revenge once they won the war. He asked Americans to help each other.

But on April 14, 1865, the nation lost its new sense of peace. **John Wilkes Booth**, an actor, shot Lincoln while he watched a play at a theater. The next day Lincoln died.

Abraham Lincoln

"With malice toward none, with charity for all, with firmness in the right as God gives us to see the right, let us strive on to finish the work we are in, to bind up the nation's wounds, to care for him who shall have borne the battle and for his widow and his orphan, to do all which may achieve and cherish a just and lasting peace among ourselves and with all nations."

Lincoln's second inaugural address

Lincoln's hope that the country would reunite without bitterness did not happen. People on both sides remained angry. Many years passed before a healing between the North and the South could begin.

Black Americans were now free from slavery. But they still had a struggle. For many more years they sought equal treatment with all other Americans.

Funeral car that carried Lincoln from the Executive Mansion to the Capitol, 1865

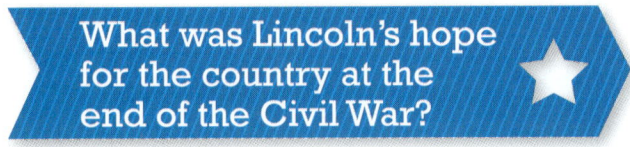

What was Lincoln's hope for the country at the end of the Civil War?

God's Grace to the Nation

The United States has received many blessings from God throughout its history. It is not a perfect nation. Like all nations, it is made up of sinful people who do sinful things. Even Christians often fail to live according to the Bible. But God has shown grace to the United States. Grace is God's favor in giving blessings that people do not deserve.

American leaders showed great wisdom in writing the Constitution. This is God's grace. God sent a revival in the early years of the nation. Many Americans became faithful Christians. This is God's grace. Natural resources filled the land. This is God's grace. Many Americans had ideas for inventions that made people's lives better. This is God's grace. And even the sad Civil War led to the end of a great national sin. This too is God's grace.

Resource Treasury

Primary Sources — 272
- Mayflower Compact — 272
- Preamble — 273
- Selection from Washington's Farewell Address — 274
- Selections from Lewis & Clark's Journals — 275
- Account about Cherokee Jesse Bushyhead — 276
- Charles Goodyear's Rubber — 277
- Selections from Eliza Spalding's Diary — 278
- Lincoln's Gettysburg Address — 279

Atlas — 280
- The United States of America: Political — 280
- The United States of America: Physical — 282

Geogloss — 284

Gazetteer — 286

Biographical Dictionary — 292

Glossary — 296

Primary Sources

Mayflower Compact

The original copy of the Mayflower Compact *was lost. But there are copies of it from the 1600s. The Pilgrims used different capitalization rules from the ones used today.*

IN THE NAME OF GOD, AMEN. We, whose names are underwritten, the Loyal Subjects of our dread Sovereign Lord King *James*, by the Grace of God, of *Great Britain*, *France*, and *Ireland*, King, *Defender of the Faith*, &c. Having undertaken for the Glory of God, and Advancement of the Christian Faith, and the Honour of our King and Country, a Voyage to plant the first Colony in the northern Parts of Virginia; Do by these Presents, solemnly and mutually, in the Presence of God and one another, covenant and combine ourselves together into a civil Body Politick, for our better Ordering and Preservation, and Furtherance of the Ends aforesaid: And by Virtue hereof do enact, constitute, and frame, such just and equal Laws, Ordinances, Acts, Constitutions, and Officers, from time to time, as shall be thought most meet and convenient for the general Good of the Colony; unto which we promise all due Submission and Obedience. **IN WITNESS** whereof we have hereunto subscribed our names at Cape-Cod the eleventh of November, in the Reign of our Sovereign Lord King James, of England, France, and Ireland, the eighteenth, and of Scotland the fifty-fourth, Anno Domini, 1620.

Benjamin Perley Poore, ed., *The Federal and State Constitutions, Colonial Charters, and Other Organic Laws of the United States, Part 1* (Washington, DC: Government Printing Office, 1878), 931.

Preamble

We the People of the United States, in order to form a more perfect union, establish justice, insure domestic tranquility, provide for the common defense, promote the general welfare, and secure the blessings of liberty to ourselves and our posterity, do ordain and establish this Constitution for the United States of America.

Selection from Washington's Farewell Address

Of all the dispositions and habits which lead to political prosperity, religion and morality are indispensable supports. In vain would that man claim the tribute of patriotism, who should labor to subvert these great pillars of human happiness, these firmest props of the duties of men and citizens. The mere politician, equally with the pious man, ought to respect and to cherish them. A volume could not trace all their connections with private and public felicity. Let it simply be asked: Where is the security for property, for reputation, for life, if the sense of religious obligation desert the oaths which are the instruments of investigation in courts of justice? And let us with caution indulge the supposition that morality can be maintained without religion. Whatever may be conceded to the influence of refined education on minds of peculiar structure, reason and experience both forbid us to expect that national morality can prevail in exclusion of religious principle.

It is substantially true that virtue or morality is a necessary spring of popular government. The rule, indeed, extends with more or less force to every species of free government. Who that is a sincere friend to it can look with indifference upon attempts to shake the foundation of the fabric?

Washington's Farewell Address 1796, The Avalon Project (New Haven, CT: Lillian Goldman Law Library, 2008).

Selections from Lewis & Clark's Journals

November 11, 1803

Arrived as Massac, engaged George Drewyer in the public service as an Indian interpreter, contracted to pay him 25 dollars per month for his services.

March 1, 1805

The same party encamped out to make the canoes, and continued until six were made.

On the 20th and 21st we carried them to the river about a mile and an half distant: There I remained with two men to finish them, and to take care of them, until the 26th, when some men came up from the fort, and we put the canoes into the water. As the river had risen there was some water between the ice and the shore. We got three of them safe to the fort; but the ice breaking before the other three were got down.

June 25, 1806

Last evening the Indians entertained us with setting the fir trees on fire. They have a great number of dry limbs near their bodies, which, when set on fire, create a very sudden and immense blaze from bottom to top of those tall trees. . . . This exhibition reminded me of a display of fireworks. The natives told us that their object in setting those trees on fire was to bring fair weather for our journey—. We collected our horses and set out at an early hour this morning. At 11 A. M. we arrived at the branch of Hungry Creek. . . . At this place the squaw collected a parcel of roots of which the Shoshones eat. It is a small knob root a good deal in flavor and consistency like the Jerusalem artichoke.

Note: Original spelling and punctuation have been modified.

Meriwether Lewis, William Clark, et al., November 11, 1803, March 1, 1805, and June 25, 1806 entries in *The Journals of the Lewis and Clark Expedition*, ed. Gary Moulton (Lincoln, NE: University of Nebraska Press / University of Nebraska-Lincoln Libraries-Electronic Text Center, 2005), http://lewisandclarkjournals.unl.edu.

Account about Cherokee Jesse Bushyhead

Four detachments of the emigrating Cherokees have, within a few days, passed through our city. . . . They average about a thousand each. . . . On Monday evening last, the 5th of November, several of them were with us, at the monthly concert of prayer for missions. . . . Brother Bushyhead, (Dta-ske-ge-de-he) addressed us in English, after prayer and a hymn in Cherokee, on the subject of missions. After pointing out the scripture authority and obligations to the holy work, he told us that he could very well remember when his nation knew nothing of Jesus Christ; he . . . illustrated the happy effects already produced among them by the Gospel. He told us he recollected most distinctly the first time he ever heard the name of the Saviour, he recounted to us some particulars of his conversion, and . . . especially of the glorious revival that prevailed among them in their camps this summer, during which himself and Ga-ne-tuh and others had baptized over a hundred and seventy. . . . He adverted to the opposition to missions waged by some Tennessee Baptists, and presented himself and hundreds of his brethren as living instances of the blessing of God upon missionary labours. He closed by stating that it was now seen that Cherokees could be christians,— commending his nation, particularly, and the Indians generally, to the prayers of the Lord's people, and beseeching them still to sustain the preaching of the Gospel among them. He set down in tears.

"The Emigrating Cherokees," *The Baptist*, December 1838, 357–58.

Charles Goodyear's Rubber

This is a description of an illuminated globe from a book by Charles Goodyear. The book is about uses for gum-elastic, or rubber.

These are made of gum-elastic tissue and vellum . . . they have a funnel made of the same material, which passes through the globe, and which is cemented to it at each pole; in the middle of the funnel is secured a fixture or cross bar, on which a lamp may be placed. The globe is thereby illuminated and becomes highly ornamental as well as useful for study at night.

Can you find the illuminated globe described above?

Charles Goodyear, *The Applications and Uses of Vulcanized Gum-Elastic; with Descriptions and Directions for Manufacturing Purposes, Vol. 2* (New Haven, CT, 1853), 36.

Selections from Eliza Spalding's Diary

Pittsburg, March 1st, 1836.

We have at length after a tedious journey of two weeks by land carriage arrived at Pittsburg, where we intend taking a steam boat for Cincinnati.

Near the Mouth of the Ohio, March 25, 1836.

In the Steam Boat Gunius.

The waters of the grand Ohio are rapidly bearing me away from all I hold dear in this life. Yet I am happy; the hope of spending . . . my life among the heathen, . . . pointing them to the Lamb of God who taketh away the sins of the world, affords me much happiness.

June 10.

I have been quite unwell for several days—and attribute my illness wholly to change of diet, which has been from necessity. Since we reached the Buffalo, our fare has been Buffalo meat.

June 14th, 1836.

Two canoes lashed together, served for our [passage]. The stream at this place is very rapid. Yesterday while the company were crossing their effects, the wind was unfavorable, and . . . several bales of goods were lost.

March 20, 1837.

The children, in particular, are interested in learning to read, several are beginning to read in the Testament. O, may this people soon have the word of God in their own language.

Eliza Spalding Warren, *Memoirs of the West* (Portland, OR: Press of the Marsh Printing Company, 1916), 55, 56, 62–63, 68–69.

Lincoln's Gettysburg Address

Four score and seven years ago our fathers brought forth on this continent, a new nation, conceived in liberty, and dedicated to the proposition that all men are created equal.

Now we are engaged in a great civil war, testing whether that nation, or any nation so conceived and so dedicated, can long endure. We are met on a great battle-field of that war. We have come to dedicate a portion of that field, as a final resting place for those who here gave their lives that that nation might live. It is altogether fitting and proper that we should do this.

But, in a larger sense, we can not dedicate—we can not consecrate—we can not hallow—this ground. The brave men, living and dead, who struggled here, have consecrated it, far above our poor power to add or detract. The world will little note, nor long remember what we say here, but it can never forget what they did here. It is for us the living, rather, to be dedicated here to the unfinished work which they who fought here have thus far so nobly advanced. It is rather for us to be here dedicated to the great task remaining before us—that from these honored dead we take increased devotion to that cause for which they gave the last full measure of devotion—that we here highly resolve that these dead shall not have died in vain—that this nation, under God, shall have a new birth of freedom—and that government of the people, by the people, for the people, shall not perish from the earth.

Atlas

United States: Political

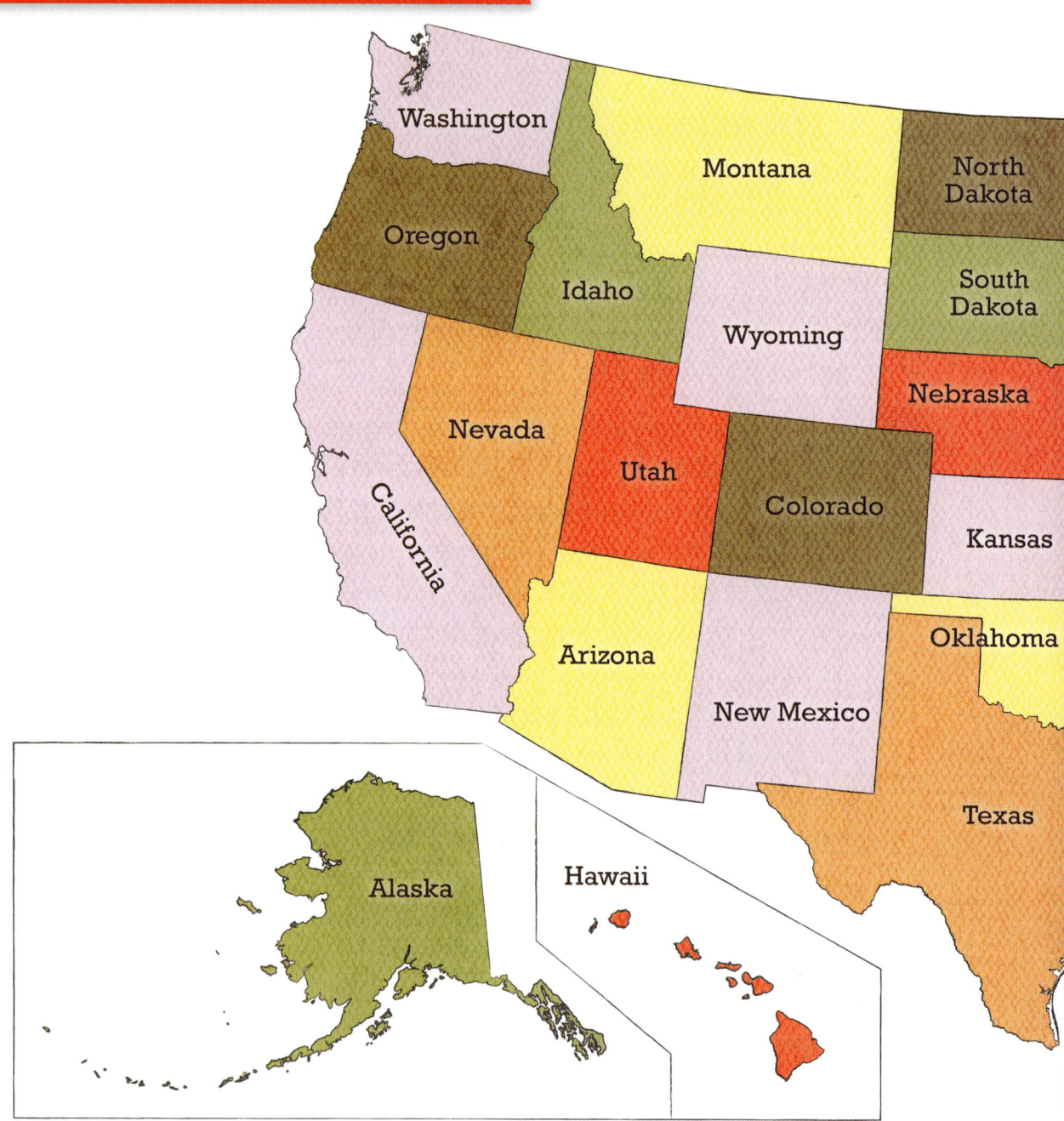

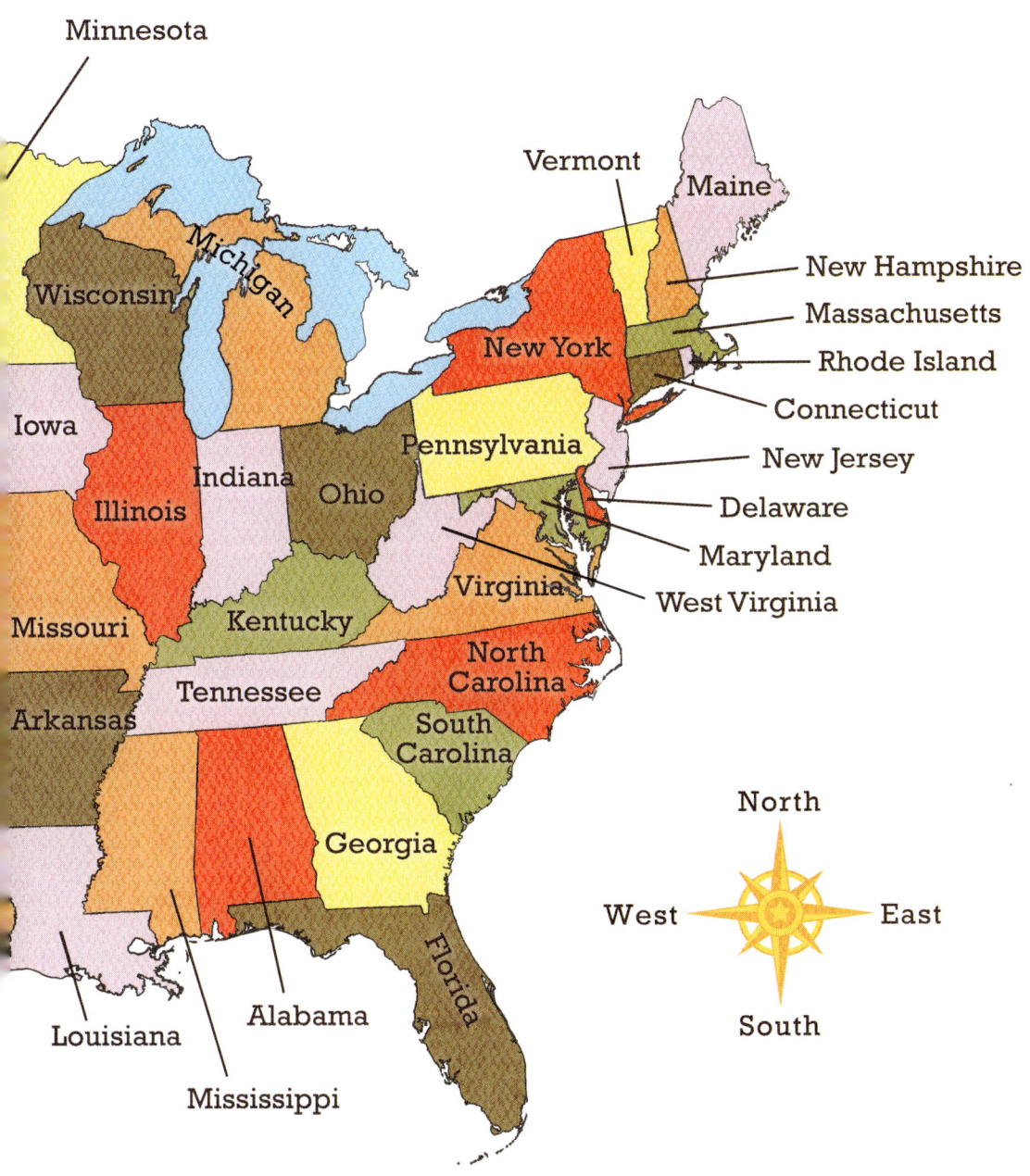

United States: Physical

Gazetteer

A gazetteer is a geographical dictionary or index. Important places from this book are listed in this gazetteer. Entries do not have complete definitions like a normal dictionary. Instead, each place is followed by helpful information you can find in this book. Many descriptions end with the page number of a map that shows that place.

A

Africa The continent that Europeans needed to sail around in order to reach India and China; the home of most slaves before they were captured and sold into slavery. (7, 147)

Alamo, the An old mission in Texas that Texan and American soldiers used as a fort; Santa Anna captured the Alamo during the Mexican-American War. (188)

Americas, the The land that makes up both North and South America.

Appomattox Court House, Virginia The location of General Lee's surrender to General Grant; the surrender ended the Civil War.

Arkansas A southern state that Union general Winfield Scott wanted to cut off from the rest of the South. (244, 248)

Asia The largest of the world's seven continents. (147)

Atlanta, Georgia The first city captured by Union general William Sherman on his march toward the seacoast.

Atlantic Ocean The ocean between Europe and America. Many inner American states are connected to the Atlantic Ocean by canals. (18–19, 125, 165)

B

Baltimore, Maryland An important port city; the site of a major battle between the British and the Americans in the War of 1812.

Bleeding Kansas The name given to the Kansas Territory as fighting over slavery spread and people were killed.

Boston, Massachusetts An important city during the Revolutionary War; home to many Irish immigrants; city Anthony Burns sailed to in an attempt to escape from slavery. (26)

Britain A powerful European country that established colonies in the New World; was ruled by a king; traded with America; fought against America in the Revolutionary War and the War of 1812. (7, 19)

Buena Vista, Mexico A village that was the site of a battle won by the Americans during the Mexican-American War. (206)

Burma A country in southeast Asia; Adoniram Judson served there as a missionary.

C

California Originally belonged to Mexico; important because of its Pacific port cities; attracted many people in the gold rush of 1849; entered United States as a free state in 1850. (201, 206, 214)

Canada A powerful British colony north of America; United States tried to take it over in the War of 1812. (30)

Caribbean A group of islands in the Caribbean Sea discovered by Columbus on his attempt to reach India and China; a source of sugar and molasses. (18)

Central America The narrow land bridge that connects Mexico and South America; a place where historians have found pyramids and carvings made by early Indian groups.

Charleston, South Carolina An important port city; site of the first battle of the Civil War. (248)

China An Asian country that traded spices and other goods with Europe.

Columbia River Located in Oregon Country. (200)

Confederate States of America The states that seceded from the United States; chose a new president and capital city; sparked the Civil War against the remaining states of the Union; often called the Confederacy. (244, 248)

D

Delaware The first state to accept the newly written Constitution. (30, 46)

E

England *See* Britain.

Erie Canal Built to connect the Great Lakes and the Atlantic Ocean; used to transport goods. (125)

Europe The continent from which most of the people in America came; European countries established colonies in new lands. (7, 19, 147)

F

Fort McHenry The fort that guarded Baltimore's harbor; successfully defended Baltimore during a British attack in the War of 1812.

Fort Sumter A US fort in South Carolina; the Confederates demanded its surrender, then attacked it; the Confederates captured the fort, starting the Civil War.

49th parallel The line of latitude that divided Oregon Country between the British and the Americans in the treaty of 1846. (200)

France A powerful European country; claimed territory and built forts in the New World; sold the Louisiana Territory to America. (7, 19, 22)

G

Georgia A slave state; home to many Cherokees before they were forced west; Union general William Sherman destroyed much of this state on his march to the seacoast. (30, 46, 149)

Gettysburg, Pennsylvania Site of a battle near the end of the Civil War; the Confederates' loss here ended their hopes of defeating the Union. (263)

Great Lakes Site of many battles between the British and Americans in the War of 1812; Britain could not keep Michigan Territory without controlling the lakes; later connected to the Atlantic Ocean by the Erie Canal. (125)

Great Plains The area between the Mississippi River and the Rocky Mountains. (191)

Great Salt Lake, Utah An area settled by Mormons in an attempt to practice their religion apart from other people.

H

Hawaii Group of islands in the Pacific Ocean where US missionaries went to tell others about Christ.

Holland A region in Europe that many immigrants in Michigan came from.

I

Illinois The first place the Mormons settled in before they continued to Utah. The state in which Abraham Lincoln lived and served in state government. (239)

India A country that traded spices and other goods with Europe; Columbus thought he found it when he sailed west and landed in the Caribbean.

Indian Territory The place that the Cherokees were forced to move to; now called Oklahoma.

Israel The area where Jesus lived; land that Christians in Europe and Muslims fought over for control. A people that God established a covenant with.

J

Jamestown The first successful English colony in the New World; traded with and was helped by the Indians. (7, 18)

K

Kansas Its people wanted to decide whether it would be a slave or free state; known as "Bleeding Kansas" after people fought and killed each other over the slavery issue. (239)

L

Lake Erie The site of a battle between the British and American navies in the War of 1812; connected to the Atlantic by the Erie Canal. (125)

Louisiana A southern state that Union general Winfield Scott wanted to cut off from the rest of the South. (244, 248)

Louisiana Territory Large area the United States bought from France in the Louisiana Purchase; President Jefferson sent the Lewis and Clark expedition to find out what this area was like. (84, 91)

M

Maine Joined the United States as a free state as part of the Missouri Compromise. (123)

Manassas, Virginia The site of two battles during the Civil War. (253)

Maryland One of the original thirteen states; state in which the Battle of Antietam was fought. (46, 253)

Massachusetts Bay Colony The Puritan settlement in the New World. (18)

Mexico The country south of America; became free from Spain in 1821; had its own constitution by 1824; fought to keep Texas and refused to sell California, but lost both in wars. (188, 201, 206)

Mexico City, Mexico The capital of Mexico; conquered by Robert E. Lee and the US Army near the end of the Mexican-American War. (206)

Michigan A state that many immigrants from Holland settled in. (173)

Michigan Territory The area from which the American army attacked the British in Canada during the War of 1812; territory was first lost to the British, then won back by the US Navy. (122, 123)

Minnesota A state that many immigrants from Norway and Sweden settled in. (173)

Mississippi River Important for trade; the western US border when Jefferson became president; linked to many states by canal; the Union wanted to capture it in the Civil War to cut off Texas, Louisiana, and Arkansas from the rest of the South. (84, 248)

Missouri Joined the nation as a slave state as part of the Missouri Compromise; people from this state voted illegally in Kansas to promote slavery. (122, 123)

Monterrey, Mexico General Taylor's capture of this city during the Mexican-American War was an important victory. (206)

N

New Hampshire The ninth state to approve the US Constitution; gave the majority needed to form the new US government. (46)

New Orleans, Louisiana A large port city at the end of the Mississippi River; controlled by Spain and then France before the United States bought it; extremely important for trade; site of the battle that occurred after the treaty of the War of 1812 was signed; was one of America's largest urban communities. (84)

New York (city) The nation's capital when Washington became president; one of America's largest urban communities; a city that Irish immigrants settled in. (65, 173)

New York (state) Did not accept the Constitution right away because it thought it could survive on its own; saw many battles between the British in Canada and the Americans in the War of 1812; built the Erie Canal. (46)

North America First settled by Indian tribes; discovered and colonized by Europeans; the first Americans to cross the entire continent were members of the Lewis and Clark expedition; the United States had spread across the continent by 1850. (7, 18)

North Carolina Did not approve the US Constitution right away because it was concerned about losing freedoms; some Civil War battles happened in this southern state. (46, 258)

North Dakota The Lewis and Clark expedition spent the winter in the area that became this state.

Norway A country that many immigrants who settled in Wisconsin and Minnesota came from.

O

Oklahoma *See* Indian Territory.

Oregon Country Land in western North America; many missionaries worked in this area; first shared by America and Britain, then divided between them along the 49th parallel. (191, 200)

P

Pacific Ocean The ocean to the west of the United States; reached by the Lewis and Clark expedition as they explored the lands west of the Mississippi River. (91, 188)

Pennsylvania Followed New York's example and built canals; General Lee attempted to capture supplies in this state during the Civil War. (125, 263)

Philadelphia, Pennsylvania A city where delegates met in 1787 to design a new government; was one of America's largest urban communities; the city Henry "Box" Brown's friends mailed him to so he could be freed from slavery. (30, 65)

Plymouth Colony The colony founded by the Pilgrims in 1620; did not have enough food or shelter for its first winter; survived with help from the Indians. (7, 18)

Potomac River A river near Washington, DC. (65, 67)

Princeton Seminary A school that was started to train pastors and to help them learn and know God's truth.

R

Rhode Island A state that did not approve the US Constitution right away because it was concerned about losing freedoms. (46)

Richmond, Virginia The capital city of the Confederate States of America. The Union army tried to defeat the Confederacy quickly by marching south to overtake this city. (248)

Rio Grande The river that flows between Texas and Mexico. (206)

Rocky Mountains A mountain range that the Lewis and Clark expedition crossed in their exploration of the Louisiana Territory. (91)

S

Saint Louis, Missouri The city where Lewis and Clark began and ended their expedition through the Louisiana Territory. (91)

San Salvador The island in the Caribbean Sea on which Columbus landed on October 12, 1492. (18)

Santa Fe, Mexico A city that was captured by the US Army at the beginning of the Mexican-American War.

Savannah, Georgia An important port city; General Sherman's destination as he fought through Georgia toward the seacoast during the Civil War. (26)

South America The continent south of North America; a place where historians have found pyramids and carvings made by early Indian groups; colonized by Europeans. (18)

South Carolina A slave state; said the tariff of 1832 was against the Constitution; the first state to secede from the United States. (239, 244)

Spain The country whose queen supported Columbus's voyage to the New World; controlled New Orleans and would not let American goods come through the city; several South American countries gained independence from Spain in the early 1800s. (7, 19)

Sweden A country that many immigrants who settled in Wisconsin and Minnesota came from.

T

Texas Land that Mexico allowed to govern itself for a time; later, fought to be free from Mexico and became an independent nation for nine years, then joined the United States as a slave state; Union general Winfield Scott tried to cut it off from the rest of the South during the Civil War. (188, 198, 201, 248)

Tower of Babel The place that all the people of the world spread out from.

Trail of Tears The path that the Cherokees traveled when they were forced to move from Georgia to the Indian Territory.

U

Union The states that chose to remain a part of the United States when southern states seceded; it had more men, factories, and railroads than the Confederacy, but had to travel south in order to fight. (244)

Utah The area to which Brigham Young led the Mormons after their first leader was killed.

V

Vancouver Island An island off the coast of Oregon Country that the British were allowed to keep when the Oregon Country was divided between Britain and the United States. (200)

Vicksburg, Mississippi The last city on the Mississippi River controlled by the Confederates during the Civil War; the site of a key Union victory. (264)

Virginia Did not approve the Constitution right away because it thought it could survive as an independent country; General Lee hoped this state would stay in the Union, but it chose to secede; site of many Civil War battles.(46, 244, 248, 250, 253)

W

Washington, DC The capital city of the United States; captured by the British during the War of 1812. (65, 67)

Wisconsin A state that many immigrants from Norway and Sweden settled in. (173)

291

Biographical Dictionary

A

Adams, Abigail Wife of John Adams; gave him wise and educated advice.

Adams, John Served as the first vice president and became the second president of the United States.

Adams, John Quincy The sixth president of the United States; son of John and Abigail Adams.

Anna, Santa A general in the Mexican army who became the president of Mexico.

B

Barton, Clara Nurse who risked her life to help the wounded during the Civil War; set up the American Red Cross.

Booth, John Wilkes The actor who shot President Abraham Lincoln.

Brown, Henry "Box" A slave who made a daring escape by mailing himself to the Anti-Slavery Society in Philadelphia.

Brown, John A man who killed five people who supported slavery in Kansas.

Buchanan, James Democratic candidate who won the presidential election of 1856 with votes from both the North and the South; had a difficult presidency.

Burns, Anthony A slave who worked in a Virginia shipyard but escaped to the North; his case went to court, and the judge ruled that Burns must be returned to his master; later some free black Americans raised enough money to buy his freedom.

Burnside, Ambrose Union general who was defeated by Lee at Fredericksburg.

C

Calhoun, John C. A politician who helped set up the American System, which included a national bank, a tariff, and improvements in transportation.

Clark, William One of the leaders of the expedition to the Louisiana Territory; knew how to lead people, make maps, and measure the land.

Clay, Henry An influential politician, secretary of state, and Speaker of the House of Representatives; helped Calhoun set up the American System.

Columbus, Christopher Explorer who discovered what is now called the Americas.

D

Davis, Jefferson President of the Confederate States of America.

Deere, John Invented the steel plow in the 1830s.

Douglas, Stephen Democratic senator from Illinois who helped convince Congress to pass the Compromise of 1850.

E

Edwards, Jonathan A Massachusetts pastor; helped spread the Great Awakening.

Eliot, John Founded towns for Indians to live in Christian communities; translated the Bible into an Indian language.

F

Fillmore, Millard President Taylor's vice president; became president when Taylor died; supported the Compromise of 1850 but opposed slavery.

Fortune, Amos Christian slave and businessman who bought his and other slaves' freedom; started a school.

Franklin, Benjamin Delegate at the Constitutional Convention; wrote a speech about the Constitution and convinced others to support it.

Fulton, Robert Steamboat company owner.

G

Gibbons, Thomas Steamboat company owner.

Goodyear, Charles Discovered a way to make rubber that did not become hard and crack in cold weather or become sticky in hot weather.

Grant, Ulysses S. Union Civil War general who captured two Confederate forts and many Confederate soldiers; later he commanded all the Union armies.

H

Hamilton, Alexander Chosen as secretary of the treasury by George Washington.

Harrison, William Henry Elected president in 1840; the first president to die while in office.

Houston, Sam Commander of the Texan army; elected president of Texas.

Howe, Elias Invented the sewing machine in the 1840s.

Hussey, Obed Invented a reaper in the early 1830s.

I

Isabella Queen of Spain who supported Columbus's trip west.

J

Jackson, Andrew General who commanded the American army in the War of 1812; seventh president of the United States.

Jackson, Thomas J. "Stonewall" Confederate general; earned his nickname by standing firm at the Battle of Bull Run.

Jay, John Sent by President Washington to Great Britain to work out an agreement with the British to leave American lands.

Jefferson, Thomas Chosen as secretary of state by George Washington; the third president of the United States.

Judson, Adoniram The first missionary from the United States to serve in a foreign country.

K

Kapiolani Member of the Hawaiian royal family who trusted Christ; had a church built for her people to learn more about God.

Key, Francis Scott Wrote the poem "The Star-Spangled Banner," which later became America's national anthem.

Knox, Henry Chosen as secretary of war by George Washington; believed the Indians had a right to their land.

L

L'Enfant, Pierre Planned the city of Washington, DC.

Lee, Robert E. Soldier who led the US Army to conquer Mexico City and defeat Santa Anna in the Mexican-American War; the South's best general during the Civil War.

Lewis, Meriwether One of the leaders of the expedition to the Louisiana Territory; knew about Indian ways and how to live in the woods.

Lincoln, Abraham President of the United States during the Civil War; shot by John Wilkes Booth.

Lincoln, Mary Todd Wife of Abraham Lincoln.

Longstreet, James General for the South during the Civil War.

M

Madison, Dolley Wife of President James Madison; saved important papers and the painting of George Washington from the White House when the British attacked.

Madison, James The fourth president of the United States; helped write the Constitution and the Bill of Rights.

Marshall, John Appointed by John Adams to be the fourth chief justice of the Supreme Court; set several precedents for the Supreme Court.

Mason, George Delegate from Virginia at the Constitutional Convention who warned about owning slaves.

McClellan, George B. Union general during the Civil War; trained the army well; was better at planning than fighting.

McCormick, Cyrus Invented a reaper, then made it better.

Monroe, James Fifth president of the United States; formed the Monroe Doctrine.

Morse, Samuel Invented the telegraph.

P

Perry, Oliver Hazard Captain who built a fleet of nine ships during the War of 1812; fought the British on Lake Erie.

Pocahontas Daughter of Indian chief Powhatan; married John Rolfe; helped the Indians and the English understand each other better.

Polk, James K. President elected in 1844; wanted more land for the United States.

Powhatan Indian chief who helped the English survive in the New World.

R

Randolph, Edmund Chosen as attorney general by Washington.

Revere, Paul Warned the Americans during the Revolutionary War that the British were coming.

Rolfe, John An important leader in Jamestown who married Pocahontas.

S

Sacagawea Indian woman who joined the Lewis and Clark expedition to the Louisiana Territory.

Samoset Indian chief who helped the Plymouth Colony survive.

Scott, Dred Slave who sued for his freedom, but the Supreme Court ruled that he remain a slave.

Scott, Winfield Union general during the Civil War; planned to win the war by setting up a blockade against the South.

Sequoyah Cherokee man who developed the written Cherokee language.

Shays, Daniel led a rebellion against the state with about 2,000 men; showed that the Articles of Confederation was weak.

Sherman, William Union general who captured Atlanta, Georgia, then marched to the seacoast; left ruin wherever he went.

Slater, Samuel Factory owner who started one of the first Sunday schools in the United States.

Smith, John Leader in Jamestown who tried to stop the fighting between the Indians and the English.

Smith, Joseph Founder of the Mormon religion.

Spalding, Henry and Eliza Missionaries to Oregon Country; built a mission to the Nez Perce Indians.

Stuart, J. E. B. Confederate general during the Civil War.

Sutter, John Owned land in California where gold was found, starting the California Gold Rush.

T

Taylor, Zachary Hero in the Mexican-American War; became president of the United States in 1848.

Trist, Nicholas Sent by President Polk to make a treaty with Mexico; asked Mexico for less land than Polk wanted.

Tubman, Harriet Helped slaves escape to freedom on the Underground Railroad.

Tyler, John Vice president to William Henry Harrison; became president when Harrison died.

V

Van Buren, Martin The eighth president of the United States.

Vanderbilt, Cornelius Steamboat company owner; offered lower prices than others; helped transportation of people and goods across America become cheaper.

W

Washington, George The first president of the United States; influenced the United States more than any other American of his time.

Wayne, Anthony Picked by Washington to train an army to fight the Indians and British in the Northwest.

Whitefield, George Preacher who traveled throughout the American colonies; helped spread the Great Awakening.

Whitman, Marcus and Narcissa Missionaries to Oregon Country; built a mission for the Cayuse Indians in 1836.

Y

York Skilled hunter and scout; William Clark's personal slave; went with the Lewis and Clark expedition to the Louisiana Territory.

Young, Brigham Mormon leader who led the entire Mormon community to the region of the Great Salt Lake in Utah.

Glossary

A

abolitionists A group of people who wanted to end slavery right away.

amendment A change to the Constitution.

American Red Cross A volunteer organization that cares for people in need; set up by Clara Barton after the Civil War.

American System James Madison's plan for a national bank, a tariff, and improvements in transportation.

ammunition Anything that can be fired from a weapon and cause harm.

apply *(past tense: applied)* The act of asking to be accepted.

Articles of Confederation A set of laws formed by the American colonies after gaining independence from Britain. These laws set up a national government for all thirteen states.

B

barter To trade goods for other goods.

Battle of Antietam Won by the Union because a Union soldier found a copy of the Confederate plans.

Battle of Bull Run Fought in Manassas, Virginia; won by the Confederates.

Battle of Fredericksburg Won by the Confederates because the Union took too long to attack, giving General Lee time to strengthen his position.

Battle of Shiloh Occurred where the Confederacy's main railroads in the West met; won by the Union.

bill 1. A statement of rules that Congress wants to become a law. 2. Amount of money owed.

bill of rights A statement of rights and freedoms; made to protect people's freedom.

blockade The act of surrounding or blocking a place to stop people and goods from entering or leaving.

blockade runners Small, light boats that slipped past the US Navy blockade to bring war supplies and food to the South.

breech-loading rifle A gun that could be loaded from the back; used during the Civil War.

budget A plan for spending and saving money.

C

cabinet People chosen by the president to give the president advice.

canal A manmade waterway that connects two bodies of water.

Capitol The building in Washington, DC, where Congress works.

chief justice The top judge of the Supreme Court.

circuit-riding preachers Men who preached in several towns and rode from town to town on a planned route.

Civil War The war between the northern and southern states; caused by disagreements on slavery and states' rights.

college 1. A school of higher learning. 2. A school students go to after high school.

commission To command.
communicate To share information.
community A place where people live and work together.
competition A contest; a test of skill and ability.
compromise An agreement that is not exactly what either side wants but what both sides can agree to.
conductor During the Civil War, a person with the Underground Railroad who knew about safe places for slaves and the best ways of escape.
Confederacy What the southern states that left the United States were called during the Civil War; also known as the Confederate States of America.
Confederate States of America The states that separated from the United States.
Confederate A citizen of the Confederate States of America.
confederation A group that pledges to work together.
county One of the parts of a state or a country.
covenant 1. An agreement. 2. In the Bible, an agreement between God and people.
creed A statement of what a church believes the Bible teaches.
culture A way of life.

D

debt Money that is owed.
defeat To beat; to win over.
delegate A person who represents a group of people.
demand The amount of goods and services that people buy.
democracy A system of government in which people have the freedom to choose; rule by the people.

Democratic-Republicans Political party; favored Thomas Jefferson's idea of a nation of farmers.
Democrats Political party; new name of the Democratic-Republicans, who continued to support President Andrew Jackson.
disputed Being argued over or being disagreed on.
divide To separate.

E

Eastern Hemisphere The half of Earth that is east of the prime meridian.
elector A person who represents a state; a member of the Electoral College.
Electoral College A group of electors (state representatives) who choose the next president.
emancipate To set free.
Emancipation Proclamation The document signed by President Lincoln that declared the southern slaves' freedom.
executive branch One part of the national government; led by the president.
expand To make or become larger.
expansion The act of expanding; an increase in size.
expedition A journey taken by a group of people for a certain purpose.
expenses Money used for goods and services.
exports Something taken out of a state or country to sell.

F

Federalists Political party; liked the Constitution; liked Alexander Hamilton's ideas of power in banking and trading.

foreign Outside of one's own country.
forty-niners People who rushed to California in search of gold. These people were named after the year of the gold rush, 1849.
49th parallel A line of latitude on the earth at 49 degrees north; the line that divided Oregon Country between the British and the Americans in the treaty of 1846.

G

Great Awakening A time when many people in America returned to true religion.
Great Compromise The agreement that divided Congress into two bodies of representatives: the House of Representatives and the Senate.

I

immigrant A person who leaves his own country to live in another country.
immoral Not doing right; choosing to do bad or wrong things.
import Something brought into a state or country to sell.
improvement The result of something that was made better.
inaugural Something connected to when someone becomes president.
inauguration The time when someone becomes president.
income Money that comes in.
indentured servant A person who pays off a debt with work instead of money.
Indian Removal Bill A statement that allowed the national government to give lands west of the Mississippi River to the Indians.

introduce 1. To make something familiar or known for the first time. 2. To make someone familiar or known to another person for the first time.
inventor Someone who makes new things or improves old things.
ironclad ship A ship with iron sides; built this way for protection during battle.

J

judicial branch The second part of the national government; led by the Supreme Court.
judicial review The idea that the Supreme Court oversees all laws and decides if the laws agree with the Constitution.
justice A judge in the United States Supreme Court.

L

legislative branch The third part of the national government; Congress.
legislature A group of representatives who pass laws.
liberty Freedom.
loft An open space under a roof; an attic.
Louisiana Purchase America's purchase from France; America bought New Orleans and the Louisiana Territory.

M

Manifest Destiny The belief that God gave the United States the right to own all the lands between the Atlantic and Pacific Oceans.
manufacturer Someone who makes goods.
manufacturing The making of goods.
Mayflower The ship the Pilgrims used to sail to the New World.

Mayflower Compact The laws that the Pilgrim leaders wrote down for their colony.
military Armed forces, such as an army and navy.
militia A group of citizens who are trained to defend their country.
miner A person who gets natural resources from the earth.
mission A place used for missionary work.
missionary Someone sent to another area or another country to teach the gospel.
Missouri Compromise The agreement that Missouri would be a free state; Congress's plan to balance the number of free and slave states. A line was drawn west of Missouri's southern border; any future state north of that border would be free, and states south of the line would be slave.
Monroe Doctrine A plan that James Monroe and John Quincy Adams made to protect the independent nations in the Americas from Europe.
Mormons A religious group that traveled west in order to practice their religion apart from other Americans.

N

natural resource Anything from nature that God created for people to use.
nonrenewable resource A natural resource that no longer forms today.
Northern Hemisphere The half of Earth that is located north of the equator.

P

pass 1. To move past something. 2. To complete with satisfying results. 3. To make lawful.
patent A right that says only the inventor may make or sell his invention.
patriotism Love and faithfulness to one's country.
petition A written request for a right from a leader.
pioneer A person who is the first to settle an area.
plantations Large farms.
political party A group of people who try to gain power in government.
port A place near a body of water where ships dock to load and unload goods.
prairie schooner Another name for a covered wagon.
preamble An introduction.
precedent An example.
primary source Something that is written or made by someone who was there when the event happened.
prime meridian A line that runs north and south on the globe; divides the Eastern and Western Hemispheres.
proclamation An official public announcement.
profit The amount of money gained after selling something for more than the amount of money paid for those goods.
progress Steady improvement; growth.

R

ratify To accept; to authorize.
reaper A machine that cuts and gathers grain.
rebel 1. Someone who goes against an authority. 2. To go against an authority.
rebellion An act against an authority.
reform A change to make something better or more just.
regiment A group of soldiers.

region An area; part of a country or part of the world.

renewable resource A natural resource that can be made again naturally.

repeating rifle A gun that could fire seven times before it needed to be reloaded; used during the Civil War.

represent To act or speak for a person or for something.

representation To be represented.

representative 1. A person who people choose to act or speak for them. 2. Someone who makes laws.

republic A balanced type of government that is run by representatives; people take part in government through them.

Republican Party A political party that formed after separating from the Whigs; wanted to protect manufacturing in the North; was against slavery.

retreat To leave.

revenge The act of harming someone to get even with them for a wrong; an act the Bible teaches not to do.

revival A time when God works and many people come to know Him.

rural community A place where people live that is outside a city; often has fewer people and more farms and land; often called the countryside.

S

savings Money that is not spent.

secede To separate; to break away as a member of a group.

secondary source Something made by someone who studied a primary source.

seminary A school that trains pastors.

settlement An area where people live and form a community.

Southern Hemisphere The half of Earth that is located south of the equator.

spending Using money for goods and services.

"Star-Spangled Banner, The" A poem by Francis Scott Key that became America's national anthem.

"Stonewall" The nickname given to General Thomas J. Jackson during the Battle of Bull Run.

supply The goods and services that a business produces.

T

tariff A tax on goods coming into a country.

telegraph A machine that used a wire to send messages in an instant.

temperance movement A plan for change by a group of people who were against alcohol and drunkenness.

term The amount of time a president serves before another election is held; four years.

territory Land owned by a national government.

Thirteenth Amendment The law that ended slavery in all the states.

thresh To separate grain from its husks.

Trail of Tears The path the Cherokees traveled when they were forced to move west.

translate To write or speak words from one language to another so someone else can understand them.

transport To move people or goods from one place to another.

transportation A way to move people or goods.

troop A group of soldiers.

U

Underground Railroad A group of people who helped runaway slaves.

Union 1. The states that did not secede from the United States. 2. What the North was called during the Civil War.

unorganized territory An area with no set government.

urban community A large community; usually called a city.

V

veto To refuse a bill.

victory 1. The act of winning. 2. Having success over the enemy.

virtue Wisdom, goodness, fairness, and morality.

voluntary society A group of volunteers who try to solve problems.

volunteer A person who works without pay.

W

Western Hemisphere The half of Earth that is west of the prime meridian.

Whig Party A political group that separated from the Democratic-Republicans and formed a new political party; thought that President Andrew Jackson took too much power.

White House The building where the president of the United States lives and works.

Index

A

abolitionist, 157–59, 233
Adams, Abigail, 75
Adams, John, 53, 71–75, 77, 79–80, 93
Adams, John Quincy, 119, 133–37, 139, 148, 158–59
Africa, 4, 7, 14, 19, 37, 227
African, 19, 159, 227
African Missionary Association, 159
Alamo, the, 189–90
amendment, 116, 118, 257
American Indians. *See* Indians
American Red Cross, 262
American System, 117
Amistad, 159
ammunition, 242, 252
Anna, Santa, 188–90, 205–6
Antietam, Battle of, 252, 254
Anti-Federalists. *See under* political party
Anti-Slavery Society, 216
Appomattox Court House, Virginia, 266
Arkansas, 248
Articles of Confederation, 29–30, 32, 35, 40–41
Asia, 11
Atlanta, Georgia, 265
Atlantic Ocean, 17, 84, 116, 125, 161, 199
attorney general, 57

B

Baltimore, Maryland, 111, 179
Baptists, 45, 56
Barbary pirates, 86–87
barter, 12
Barton, Clara, 262
battles. *See names of individual battles, e.g., Fallen Timbers, Battle of*
bill, 35, 43, 118, 150, 214–16
Bill of Rights, 44–45, 103, 158
black Americans, 14, 89, 131, 141, 159, 169, 218, 223, 226–27, 232, 238, 256, 268
Bleeding Kansas, 222
blockade, 247, 258–59, 262
blockade runner, 258
Booth, John Wilkes, 267
Boston, Massachusetts, 25, 173, 218
breech-loading rifle, 260
Britain, 20, 22–23, 27, 29, 37, 62–63, 104–7, 110–13, 116, 128, 131
British, 22–23, 25, 27, 62, 104–12, 114, 116, 133, 196, 199–200
Brown, Henry "Box," 216
Brown, John, 157, 222, 233
Buchanan, James, 234
budget, 60
Buena Vista, Battle of, 205
Bull Run, Battle of, 249–50, 252
Burma, 145
Burns, Anthony, 218–19
Burnside, Ambrose, 252–53

C

cabinet, 57, 119, 254
Calhoun, John C., 117, 154–55, 213
California, 201–2, 204, 209–11, 214, 220
Canada, 105, 107–8, 110, 112
canal, 79, 116–18, 121, 125–27, 136, 161, 164–65, 167, 174
capital, 65–67, 71, 108, 111, 206, 241, 248, 252, 253, 264, 266
Capitol, 67, 94, 268
Caribbean, 5, 18, 19
Catholics, 188
Cayuse, 192
Charleston, South Carolina, 169, 242
Cherokees, 120, 148–51
chief justice, 92–93
China, 4, 5
Christianity, 3, 5, 54, 96, 98, 144–45
church, 9, 15, 20–21, 27, 54, 56, 67, 78, 96–98, 124, 141, 143–46, 148, 180, 189, 193, 227, 231

Church of England, 15
circuit-riding preachers, 56
citizen, 33, 41, 50, 131, 148, 223, 238, 242–43, 256
city council, 64
Civil War, 38, 242, 246, 253, 255, 257–58, 260, 262, 269
Clark, William, 88–91
Clay, Henry, 117, 134–35, 155, 198, 214–15
college, 66, 67, 97, 136
colony, 7, 9, 21, 22, 107, 119
Columbia River, 200
Columbus, Christopher, 5–7, 11, 67
commission, 2
communication, 124, 177, 179, 181, 184, 261
community, 12, 41, 64, 97–98, 124–25, 142, 174
compromise, 36, 42, 123, 215, 233
Compromise of 1850, 214–16, 219
conductors, 217
Confederacy, 245–46, 248, 251, 258, 266
Confederates, 242, 246, 249–53, 256, 259, 264
Confederate States of America, 241–42, 244–45, 254–55, 262
confederation, 241
Congress, 34–38, 45, 59, 64–65, 68, 85, 92, 94, 103–4, 115–18, 122–23, 136, 154–55, 158, 177, 196, 198, 203–4, 207, 213–15, 221, 237, 257
constitution, 42, 47
    Cherokee Constitution, 148
    Mexican Constitution, 187–88, 190
    state constitution, 33
    United States Constitution, 32, 34–35, 39–47, 59, 74, 94, 103, 116, 118, 136, 148, 154–55, 223, 238, 254, 257, 269
Constitutional Convention, 32–34, 42, 49
Continental Congress, 25
cotton, 19, 37, 81, 83, 120–21, 129, 168–69, 183, 228, 247, 258
covenant, 16
creed, 143
Creeks, 113, 120
CSS *Virginia*, 259
culture, 11, 15, 176, 225

D

Davis, Jefferson, 241–42
debt, 14, 31, 66, 70
Deere, John, 171
Delaware, 46
delegate, 32–34, 36–39, 42–43
demand, 162–63
democracy, 77, 79–80, 95–98, 140–42, 144, 176, 210
Democratic-Republicans. *See under* political party
Democrats. *See under* political party
Douglas, Stephen, 215, 220–21, 235–36

E

Edwards, Jonathan, 21
election, 31, 95, 103, 133, 137, 196, 198, 208, 222, 234, 236, 238
Election of 1800, 75, 77, 80
elector, 51, 71
Electoral College, 51, 133, 137
Eliot, John, 12
emancipate, 254–55
Emancipation Proclamation, 254–57
England, 7, 9, 10, 15, 20, 86, 129
English, 7–8, 9, 10
Erie Canal, 79, 116, 125
Europe, 3–4, 7, 14, 18, 121, 173
European, 4–7, 13, 18–19, 87, 113, 119, 121, 177
Evangelical Christians, 55–56
executive branch, 34, 57, 68
expedition, 88
expenses, 60
explorer, 7, 67, 90, 202
export, 38–39, 120

F

factory, 39, 115–17, 121, 129–31, 162, 169–70, 174, 224, 225, 245, 258
Fallen Timbers, Battle of, 62
Federalists. *See under* political party
Fillmore, Millard, 215
foreign, 145

Fort McHenry, 111, 114
Fort Sumter, 242–43
Fortune, Amos, 14
forty-niners, 209
49th parallel, 200
France, 22, 73, 85–86, 104, 106, 111
Franklin, Benjamin, 42
Fredericksburg, Battle of, 252
freedom, 14, 27, 29, 41, 43–44, 47, 53, 77–78, 87, 96, 100, 107, 158, 159, 176, 189, 216–18, 221, 223, 225, 256
    of religion, 9, 45, 78, 141–42, 158
    of speech, 74, 158
Fremont, John C., 202
French, 22–23, 84, 104
Fulton, Robert, 126, 163

G

Georgia, 37, 149–50, 265
German, 174
Gettysburg, Battle of, 262
Gibbons, Thomas, 163
Golden Rule, 226
gold rush, 209
goods, 4, 6, 12, 38–39, 60, 62, 78, 81, 84, 86, 104, 115–16, 121, 125–30, 161–67, 169, 184, 209, 251–52
Goodyear, Charles, 171–72
government, 9, 15, 24, 34, 40, 47, 50, 70, 75, 87
    British, 9, 23–24, 44
    Confederate, 245
    local, 63–64, 210
    Mexican, 187–88
    national, 29–32, 34, 35, 39–41, 43–44, 54, 57, 60, 61, 63–66, 104, 116, 121, 150, 177, 197, 213, 220, 223
    Spanish, 159
    state, 29, 31, 34, 38, 63–64, 80, 125, 222, 235
    US, 9, 27, 33–35, 42, 44, 46–47, 49, 57, 59, 61, 71–72, 74, 77–80, 92–93, 95, 98, 104, 113, 117, 120, 133, 137–41, 150, 152, 172, 179, 210
governor, 22, 196, 242

Grant, Ulysses S., 251, 261, 264–66
Great Awakening, 20–22
Great Britain. *See* Britain
Great Commission, 3
Great Compromise, 36
Great Lakes, 108, 110, 116, 125
Great Plains, 191
Great Salt Lake, 195

H

Hamilton, Alexander, 57–60, 65–66, 72
Harrison, William Henry, 196–97
Hawaii, 145–46
Hawaiians, 146
Holland, 173
House of Representatives, 36, 133–34, 235
Houston, Sam, 190
Howe, Elias, 171
Hussey, Obed, 171

I

Illinois, 194, 220–21, 235
immigrant, 173–76, 181
import, 38–39, 115–16, 154, 247
income, 60
indentured servant, 14
India, 3–6
Indiana, 125
Indian Removal Bill, 150
Indians, 5–8, 10–13, 22–23, 61–63, 88–90, 105, 107, 110, 113, 131, 141, 145, 148–50, 191–93
Indian Territory, 151
invention, 126–27, 171–72, 179–81, 184–85, 260, 269
inventor, 66, 126, 167, 171–72, 178–79, 184, 260
Ireland, 174
Irish, 173–74
ironclad ship, 259
Isabella (queen of Spain), 5
Islam, 3
Israel, 3, 5, 16, 227, 231

J

Jackson, Andrew, 112–13, 133–40, 148–53, 155–56, 190
Jackson, Thomas J. "Stonewall," 246, 249, 252
Jamestown, 7–8
Jay, John, 62
Jefferson, Thomas, 55–60, 65–66, 71–72, 74, 77–81, 84–88, 92, 99–101, 103, 187
judge, 34–35, 92–93, 218
judicial branch, 34
judicial review, 94
Judson, Adoniram, 145
justice, 92–94

K

Kansas, 222
Kapiolani, 145–46
Kentucky, 235
Key, Francis Scott, 114
king, 9, 25, 50, 153
Knox, Henry, 57, 61

L

Lake Erie, 110, 116
language, 8, 12, 27, 89–90, 145, 148, 193
law, 9, 16, 23–24, 29, 31–35, 41–43, 46, 57–58, 64, 74, 94, 113, 116, 118, 134, 149–50, 152, 154–55, 159, 188, 204, 210, 216, 222, 235
lawmaker, 23, 235
lawyer, 114, 159, 235
Lee, Robert E., 206, 247–48, 252–53, 262, 264, 266
legislative branch, 34
legislature, 64
L'Enfant, Pierre, 67
Lewis, Meriwether, 88
Lewis and Clark expedition, 88–89, 91
Lexington and Concord, Battle of, 25
liberty, 41, 53, 232
Lincoln, Abraham, 221, 232, 235–38, 241–44, 249–50, 252, 254–57, 264, 266–68
local government. *See under* government
Longstreet, James, 246

Louisiana, 248
Louisiana Purchase, 85, 88
Louisiana Territory, 84–85, 88, 122

M

Madison, Dolley, 114
Madison, James, 34–35, 45, 74, 103–5, 113, 115–19
Maine, 123
Manassas, Virginia, 249
Manifest Destiny, 199
manufacturer, 116–17, 154, 170
manufacturing, 39, 121–22, 169, 236
Marshall, John, 92–94
Maryland, 66, 227, 252
Mason, George, 37–38
Massachusetts, 21, 32, 45, 54, 115, 123
Massachusetts Bay Colony, 15
Mayflower, 9–10, 17
Mayflower Compact, 9, 17
mayor, 64
McClellan, George B., 250, 252
McCormick, Cyrus, 171–72
Methodists, 55–56, 227
Mexico, 187–88, 190, 200–208, 211
    government, 187–88 Mexican-American War, 203–6, 208–9, 213
    Mexican Constitution, 187–88, 190
    Mexicans, 188, 201–2, 204–5, 208–9
    Mexico City, 203, 206
Michigan, 173
Michigan Territory, 108, 110
military, 57–58, 86, 108, 115
militia, 243
miner, 209–10
Minnesota, 173
mission, 189, 191–93
missionary, 97, 141, 145–46, 150, 159, 180, 191, 193
Mississippi, 251
Mississippi River, 62, 81, 84–85, 148, 150, 161, 187, 211, 245, 248, 251, 264
Missouri, 122–23, 222
Missouri Compromise, 122–23, 220
Missouri River, 89

Monroe, James, 119–20, 148
Monroe Doctrine, 119
Monterrey, Mexico, 205
Mormons, 194–95
Morse, Samuel, 178–79
Morse code, 261
Muslims, 3–5

N

national anthem, 114
national bank, 59–60, 115, 117, 152
national government. *See under* government
natural resource, 81–83, 131, 209, 211, 269
New Hampshire, 46, 130
New Jersey, 143, 163
New Orleans, Battle of, 112
New Orleans, Louisiana, 63, 84–85, 112, 124, 169
newspaper, 74, 124, 137, 148, 150, 158, 167, 179, 194, 199, 233, 235
New York (city), 65, 173
New York (state), 39, 47, 108, 112, 116, 124–25, 158, 159, 163
Nez Perce, 193
nonrenewable resource, 83
North America, 11–12, 14–15, 20, 22–23, 90, 199, 211
North Carolina, 47, 266
North Dakota, 90
Northwest Territory, 100
Norway, 173

O

Ohio, 125
Oklahoma, 151
"Old Ironsides," 109
Olmecs, 11
Oregon Country, 191–93, 199–200

P

Pacific Ocean, 88, 90, 199
pastor, 21, 27, 45, 96–98, 142–44, 180, 207, 229
patent, 172
patriotism, 114
Pele, 146

Pennsylvania, 42, 125, 141, 262
Perry, Oliver Hazard, 110
petition, 25, 158
Philadelphia, Pennsylvania, 32–33, 60, 117, 124, 152, 216
Pilgrims, 9–10, 15
pioneer, 192
plantation, 19, 37, 50, 100, 121, 168, 228, 230–31
Plimoth Plantation, 17
Plymouth Colony, 9–10
Pocahontas, 8
political party, 70–72, 74, 77, 80, 94, 153, 234
    Anti-Federalists, 43–45
    Democratic-Republicans, 72–73, 77, 80–81, 92–93, 95, 103, 105–6, 120, 153
    Democrats, 153, 196–99, 234, 236
    Federalists, 43, 72–73, 77, 79–80, 92, 95, 153
    Republicans, 234, 236
    Whigs, 153, 196–98, 208, 234
Polk, James K., 198–204, 206–8, 211
port, 111, 169, 201–2, 247, 258
postal service, 124
postmaster, 157
post office, 124, 177, 180
Potomac River, 66
Powhatan, 7–8
prairie schooner, 195
preacher, 21, 56, 146, 180
preamble, 40–41
precedent, 49, 68–69, 80, 92–93
president, 34–35, 49–51, 57, 64, 67–69, 71, 80, 92–93, 133–35, 137, 139, 150, 153, 196–97, 236–37, 254
    Adams, John, 71, 77, 80, 93
    Adams, John Quincy, 134, 137, 139
    Anna, Santa, 188
    Buchanan, James, 234
    Davis, Jefferson, 241, 242
    Fillmore, Millard, 215, 218
    Harrison, William Henry, 196–97
    Houston, Sam, 190
    Jackson, Andrew, 137–39, 148–50, 156, 190

Jefferson, Thomas, 71, 77, 80, 84, 92, 103, 187
Lincoln, Abraham, 235, 237–38, 241, 249, 256–57, 264, 266–67
Madison, James, 103–4, 113–14, 118–19
Monroe, James, 119
Polk, James K., 198–99, 203, 211
Taylor, Zachary, 208, 213–15
Tyler, John, 197
Van Buren, Martin, 156, 159, 196
Washington, George, 49–52, 57, 60, 65, 67–69, 70
primary sources, 17
Princeton Seminary, 143
proclamation, 254
profit, 4–7
Puritans, 15–16, 20

R

railroad, 127, 164–67, 184, 220, 245, 251, 260, 265
Randolph, Edmund, 57
reaper, 171–72, 184
rebellion, 29, 32, 41, 98, 159
reform, 181–83
regiment, 256
religion, 3, 12, 21, 47, 53–56, 78, 80, 97–98, 141–42, 144, 188, 195
"Remember the Alamo!," 190
renewable resource, 83
repeating rifle, 260
representative, 24–25, 33–36, 64, 123
republic, 33
Republicans. *See under* political party
Revere, Paul, 25
revival, 21, 47, 55–56, 96, 269
Revolutionary War, 24–27, 29, 31, 41, 44–45, 49, 66, 141, 148
Rhode Island, 47, 129
Richmond, Virginia, 241, 245, 248–50, 253, 264, 266
Rio Grande, 203
Rocky Mountains, 90
Rolfe, John, 8
rubber, 11, 171

rural community, 124–25

S

Sacagawea, 90
Saint Louis, Missouri, 89, 91
Samoset, 10
San Jacinto, Battle of, 190
San Salvador, 5
Santa Fe, Mexico, 204
Savannah, Georgia, 169
savings, 60
school, 14, 61, 96, 124, 131, 141–43, 146, 192–93, 235
Scott, Dred, 223–24
Scott, Winfield, 202, 247–48
secede, 238, 241–43, 247, 254
secondary sources, 17
secretary of state, 57, 119, 135
secretary of the treasury, 57, 152
secretary of war, 57
seminary, 143
Senate, 36, 235
Sequoyah, 148
settlement, 15, 16, 61, 126, 191
sewing machine, 171, 183
Shays, Daniel, 32
Shays' Rebellion, 32, 41
Sherman, William, 265–66
Shiloh, Battle of, 251
Slater, Samuel, 131
slave, 14, 19, 37–38, 86, 89, 100–101, 120, 141, 159, 168–69, 188, 210, 213–14, 216–21, 223–34, 237–38, 241, 247, 254–56
slavery, 14, 37–38, 97, 100–101, 121, 157–59, 182, 188, 213–15, 219–27, 229–30, 232–34, 236–37, 254–55, 257, 268
Smith, John, 8
Smith, Joseph, 194
South America, 11
South Carolina, 37, 154–55, 238, 242
Spain, 5–6, 10, 62–63, 119, 187
Spalding, Henry and Eliza, 193
speech, 42, 52, 69–70, 267
spirituals, 231
Squanto, 10

"Star-Spangled Banner, The," 114
state government. *See under* government
steamboat, 126–27, 162–66, 177, 184
steam engine, 126–27, 170
steel plow, 171
Stuart, J. E. B., 246
Sunday school, 131
supply, 162–63, 209
Supreme Court, 34–35, 92–94, 150, 159, 163, 223
Sutter, John, 209
Sweden, 173

tariff, 38–39, 115–17, 121–22, 154–55
taxes, 23–24, 29, 31, 38, 60, 96, 98, 115, 136
Taylor, Zachary, 203, 205, 208, 213–15
Tecumseh, 110
telegraph, 178–79, 180, 184–85, 261
temperance movement, 181–82
term, 69, 103, 118–19, 156, 267
territory, 64, 122, 213–14, 220–21, 223, 232–33, 236–37, 254
Texas, 187–90, 197–98, 201–3, 205, 248
Thirteenth Amendment, 256–57
thresh, 167
Todd, Mary, 235
tower of Babel, 11
trade, 4, 7, 12, 18, 20, 38–39, 61, 72, 84–86, 90, 104–5, 107, 115, 117, 121, 125–26, 128, 166, 199
trader, 78–79, 89
tradition, 176
Trail of Tears, 151
train, 126–27, 164, 166, 177, 249, 260
translate, 12, 90, 145
transportation, 81, 115–18, 124–28, 161, 163–64, 166, 177, 181, 184–85
treaty, 27, 85, 110, 112–13, 148, 150–51, 200, 208–9, 211
Trist, Nicholas, 208
Tubman, Harriet, 217
Tyler, John, 196–97

U

Underground Railroad, 217

Union, 199, 245, 247–56, 258–59, 261–62, 264–65
urban community, 124–25
USS *Constitution*, 109–10
Utah, 194–95

V

Van Buren, Martin, 156–57, 159, 196
Vancouver Island, 200
Vanderbilt, Cornelius, 163
veto, 118
vice president, 71, 156, 196–97, 215
Vicksburg, Mississippi, 264
Virginia, 22, 37, 45–47, 92, 218, 223, 247, 250, 252, 262, 264
voluntary society, 97–98, 142, 181
volunteer, 166, 181–82, 189, 250
vote, 35, 42, 45–46, 51, 71, 80, 85, 95, 122, 133–34, 137, 159, 214–15, 220, 222, 232, 234, 236–38, 255
voter, 33, 51

War for Independence, 25
War of 1812, 106–8, 114–15, 120, 128–29, 131, 133, 148
Washington, DC, 66–67, 92, 111, 114, 136, 179, 249
Washington, George, 22, 25, 32, 42, 49–53, 57–62, 65–72, 75, 103, 114
Wayne, Anthony, 62–63
wealth, 20, 72
weapons, 7, 14, 18, 32, 62, 105, 107, 242
whaling, 128
"What hath God wrought," 179
Whigs. *See under* political party
Whitefield, George, 20–21
White House, 111, 114, 138, 208
Whitman, Marcus and Narcissa, 191–93
Wisconsin, 173

Y

York, 89
Yorktown, Battle of, 25, 27
Young, Brigham, 195

Photograph Credits

Key
(t) top; (c) center;
(b) bottom; (l) left; (r) right

Chapter 1

5 ©iStockphoto.com/SlidePix; **9** SuperStock /SuperStock; **10** ©iStockphoto.com/capecodphoto; **12** Three Lions/Stringer/Hulton Archive/Getty Images; **16** © North Wind Picture Archives / Alamy; **17t** AP Photo/Daily Press, Joe Fudge; **17b** Tim Graham/Getty Images News/Getty Images; **20** John Collet/The Bridgeman Art Library/Getty Images; **21t** "Jonathan Edwards engraving" by R Babson & J Andrews/Wikimedia Commons/Public Domain; **21b** "George Whitefield preaching"/Wikimedia Commons/Public Domain; **23** "Proof sheet of one penny stamps Stamp Act 1765" by Board of Stamps/Wikipedia/Public Domain; **25** "Surrender of Lord Cornwallis" by John Trumbull/Wikimedia Commons/Public Domain

Chapter 2

29 "Articles page1"/Wikimedia Commons/Public Domain; **31** (all) iStockphoto/Thinkstock; **32** Courtesy of Mount Vernon Ladies' Association; **33** ©iStockphoto.com/JacobH; **37** "Slave ship diagram"/Wikimedia Commons/Public Domain; **39** Nicholas Pocock/The Bridgeman Art Library/Getty Images; **40** "Scene at the Signing of the Constitution of the United States" by Howard Chandler Christy/Wikipedia/Public Domain; **41** (all) "Constitution of the United States"/U.S. National Archives and Records Administration/Wikipedia/Public Domain; **42t** spirit of america /Shutterstock.com; **42b** Visions of America /SuperStock; **43** "Federalist Papers"/Wikipedia/Public Domain; **44** © Boris Hudak | Dreamstime.com; **45** Britannica Kids/Public Domain

Chapter 3

49 "Gilbert Stuart Williamstown Portrait of George Washington" by Gilbert Stuart/Wikipedia/Public Domain; **50** "Junius Brutus Stearns - George Washington as Farmer at Mount Vernon" by Junius Brutus Stearns/Wikipedia/Public Domain; **52t** The Colonial Williamsburg Foundation; **52b** MANDEL NGAN/Staff/AFP/Getty Images; **53** "Jadams" by John Trumbull/Wikipedia/Public Domain; **54l** "Old Ship Church Redux" by Old Ship Church Redux/Flickr/CC-By-SA 2.0; **54r** "InteriorOldShip" by Michael Carter/Wikimedia Commons/CC-By-SA 2.0; **55** Library of Congress, LC-USZC4-772; **56** Library of Congress, LC-USZC4-6153; **60** Nikhilesh Haval / age fotostock / SuperStock; **62** Buyenlarge / SuperStock; **63** "American Legion 1794"/Wikimedia Commons/Public Domain; **66** © John Kropewnicki | Dreamstime.com; **67** "L'Enfant plan"/Library of Congress/Wikipedia/Public Domain; **68** © Songquan Deng | Dreamstime.com; **69** "George Washington's Farewell Address"/Public Domain; **71** "US Navy 031029-N-6236G-001 A painting of President John Adams (1735-1826), 2nd president of the United States, by Asher B. Durand (1767-1845)"/Wikipedia/Public Domain; **74t** "1799 MassachusettsMercury Boston Dec24"/Wikimedia Commons/Public Domain; **74b** © Romica | Dreamstime.com; **75** "Abigail Smith Adams" by Gilbert Stuart/Wikimedia Commons/Public Domain

Chapter 4

78 "Edward Hicks - The Cornell Farm"/Wikimedia Commons/Public Domain; **79** North Wind Picture Archives via AP Images; **83**tl ©iStockphoto.com/Petek ARICI; **83**tr, **83**cl, **94**r, **99**tr, **99**cbr iStockphoto/Thinkstock; **83**cr ©iStockphoto.com/Elena Elisseeva; **83**bl © Tengu - Fotolia.com; **83**br ©iStockphoto.com/Roadrunnerdeluxe; **85**t, b Courtesy National Archives; **86** "NH 65536-KN"/U.S. Naval Academy Museum/Wikimedia Commons/Public Domain; **87** "EnterpriseTripoli"/Wikimedia Commons/Public Domain; **88**t, c National Park Service; **88**b, **89** Lewis and Clark at Three Forks, E.S. Paxson, Oil on Canvas, 1912, Montana Historical Society, Montana State Capitol Art Collection, X1912.07.01, Don Beatty photographer 10/1999; **90** "Lewis and Clark Expedition Maps"/Wikimedia Commons/Public Domain; **92** "John Marshall by Henry Inman, 1832"/Wikimedia Commons/Public Domain; **94**l "Capitol1846" by John Plumbe/Wikipedia/Public Domain; **95** "Election Day 1815 by John Lewis Krimmel"/Wikimedia Commons/Public Domain; **97** Library of Congress, LC-USZ62-2443; **99**b ©Thomas Jefferson Foundation at Monticello, photograph by Leonard Phillips.; **99**ctr ©iStockphoto.com/Anthony Rosenberg; **99**br © Picalotta | Dreamstime.com; **101** "Isaac Jefferson c1845"/Wikipedia/Public Domain

Chapter 5

104 The Mariners' Museum, Newport News, VA; **105**l "Act of June 18, 1812, 2 STAT 755, Declaration of War with Great Britain, War of 1812. - NARA - 299950"/Wikimedia Commons/Public Domain; **105**r "Proclamation Province of Upper Canada by Isaac Brock"/Wikipedia/Public Domain; **106** Library of Congress, LC-DIG-pga-01891; **107** Library and Archives Canada, Acc. No. 1954-153-1; **108** Walter Bibikow/AWL Images/Getty Images; **109** "USS Constitution v HMS Guerriere" by Anton Otto Fischer/Wikimedia Commons; **111** Greg Pease/Photographer's Choice/Getty Images; **112** "Battle of New Orleans Jean-Hyacinthe Laclotte"/Wikimedia Commons/Public Domain; **113** "Signing of Treaty of Ghent (1812)"/Wikipedia/Public Domain; **115** "Boston Manufacturing Company mill complex, Waltham, MA - 2"/Wikimedia Commons/Public Domain; **116** North Wind Picture Archives via AP Images; **117** age fotostock / SuperStock; **119** "Flickr - USCapitol - The Monroe Doctrine, 1823"/Wikimedia Commons/Public Domain; **120** © Danny Hooks | Dreamstime.com; **126**t "Clermont (steamboat)"/Wikimedia Commons/Public Domain; **126**b SuperStock / SuperStock; **129** © Dan Logan | Dreamstime.com; **130** Public Domain

Chapter 6

135tl "Andrew Jackson Portrait2"/Wikimedia Commons/Public Domain; **135**tr Hulton Archive/Stringer/Archive Photos/Getty Images; **135**bl Kean Collection/Archive Photos/Getty Images; **135**br "Henry Clay Lafosse2"/Wikimedia Commons/Public Domain; **138**t "First Capitol Inauguration, 1829"/Flickr/Public Domain; **138**b "Jackson inauguration crop"/Wikimedia Commons/Public Domain; **141** "Sioux boys as they were dressed on arrival at the Carlisle Indian School, Pennsylvania, 10-05-1879 - NARA - 519135"/Wikimedia Commons/Public Domain; **142** Courtesy New York State Museum, Albany, NY; **143** Princeton University Library; **144** Public Domain; **145** Library of Congress, LC-USZ62-38296; **148** North Wind Picture Archives via AP Images; **151** SuperStock / SuperStock; **152** MKL/Bigstock.com; **154** "John C. Calhoun"/Wikimedia Commons/Public Domain; **156**t age fotostock / SuperStock; **156**b "The times panic 1837"/Wikipedia/Public Domain; **157** "What is life or rest to me! So long as I have a commission direct from God Almighty to act against slavery! (7645379730)"/Wikimedia Commons/CC-By-SA 2.0; **158** Library of Congress, LC-DIG-ppmsca-19705; **159** "La Amistad (ship) restored"/Wikipedia/Public Domain

Chapter 7

163 "Constitution (steamboat 1825)" by Samuel Ward Stanton/Wikimedia Commons/Public Domain; **164** Library of Congress; **170** ©iStockphoto.com/duncan1890; **171**t ©iStockphoto.com/fotosmania; **171**c ©iStockphoto.com/duncan1890; **171**b © Old Paper Studios / Alamy; **172** Wisconsin Historical Society, WHS-3426; **178**t "Samuel Morse 1840"/Wikimedia Commons/Public Domain; **178**b Underwood Archives/Archive Photos/Getty Images; **181** Picture Collection, The New York Public Library, Astor, Lenox and Tilden Foundations; **182** © Everett Collection Inc / Alamy; **183** ©iStockphoto.com/DougMcPhoto

Chapter 8

190 Public Domain; **192**t, b Peter Stackpole/Time & Life Pictures/Getty Images; **196** "William Henry Harrison by James Reid Lambdin, 1835-crop"/The White House Historical Association/Wikimedia Commons/Public Domain; **197** "John Tyler"/Wikimedia Commons/Public Domain; **198** "James Knox Polk by George Peter Alexander Healy, 1846 - DSC03258"/Wikimedia Commons/Public Domain; **202** Library of Congress, LC-USZC4-2955; **203** "Batalla de chapultepec - 13 de septiembre de 1847"/Wikimedia Commons/Public Domain; **204** iStockphoto/Thinkstock; **205** "Nebel Mexican War 03 Battle of Buena Vista"/Wikimedia Commons/Public Domain; **209** Library of Congress, LC-USZ62-137164; **210** "San-Francisco1851a"/Wikimedia Commons/Public Domain

Chapter 9

216 Public Domain; **218** SuperStock / SuperStock; **221** English School/The Bridgeman Art Library/Getty Images; **222** North Wind Picture Archives via AP Images; **223** "DredScott" by Louis Schultze/Missouri History Museum/Wikimedia Commons/Public Domain; **226** "Hermitage Slave Quarters (Savannah, Georgia)" by Wilson & Havens/Wikimedia Commons/Public Domain; **227** "Portrait of a Gentleman, Joshua Johnson paints Coker, 1805"/Wikimedia Commons/Public Domain; **230, 231, 232** Library of Congress; **235** © Todd Taulman | Dreamstime.com; **237** "Flickr - USCapitol - Abraham Lincoln's First Inauguration"/Wikimedia Commons/Public Domain

Chapter 10

243 Library of Congress, LC-USZC4-528; **247** Library of Congress, LC-DIG-ppmsca-35446; **249** "Jackson-Stonewall-LOC"/Wikimedia Commons/Public Domain; **251** Library of Congress, LC-DIG-cwpb-07310; **254** Library of Congress, LC-DIG-pga-02502; **255, 262** National Archives; **256** "DutchGapb"/Wikimedia Commons/Public Domain; **257** MPI/Stringer/Archive Photos/Getty Images; **259** "The Monitor and Merrimac" by Jo Davidson/Louis Prang & Co./Wikimedia Commons; **260** "Spencer rifle diagram"/Scientific American/Wikimedia Commons/Public Domain; **265** "Sherman railroad destroy" by George N. Barnard/Wikimedia Commons/Public Domain; **266** National Geographic / SuperStock; **267** Library of Congress, LC-DIG-ppmsca-23718; **268** Library of Congress, DIG-ppmsca-23860

Resource Treasury

270tl ©/iStockphoto.com/brytta; **270**tr iStockphoto/Thinkstock; **270**bl ©iStockphoto.com/Anita Stizzoli; **270**br © Edwin Wood | Dreamstime.com; **277** Illustration by Charles Goodyear/Public Domain

All maps from Map Resources